NICHOL

LOND

ATLAS & GUIDE

CONTENTS

A Nicholson Guide
© Nicholson 1996

First published 1993
2nd edition 1996

Design by Bob Vickers

Photographs by Oliver Hewitt on pages 4, 5, 8, 10, 11, 12, 13, 21, 24, 26, 28, 30, 31, 32, 33, 35, 38, 39, 40, 41, 53, 57.

Photographs by Nick Daly on pages 4, 6, 7, 11, 17, 25, 26, 27, 28, 30, 32, 34, 61.

All photographs © Nicholson with the exception of the following which have been reproduced by kind permission of the copyright holders: p19 Museum of the Moving Image; p20 Natural History Museum; p23 Tate Gallery; p51 The South Bank Centre; p52 London Coliseum, photographed by Tim Flach.

River maps, pages 30-35, by Dominic Beddow, Draughtsman Maps.

Maps © Nicholson, generated from the Bartholomew London Digital Database.
All entries in the guide are referenced to the Street Maps on pages 66-105.
The first figure is the page number, the letter and number the grid reference
on that page.

The Ordnance Survey is not responsible for the accuracy of the National Grid
on this publication.

London Underground Map reproduced by permission of London Regional Transport.
LRT Registered User No: 96/1496

Nicholson
An Imprint of HarperCollins*Publishers*
77-85 Fulham Palace Rd
Hammersmith
London W6 8JB

Great care has been taken throughout this book to be accurate, but the
publishers cannot accept responsibility for any errors which appear,
or their consequences.

Printed in Hong Kong

ISBN 0 7028 3151 4

93/2/210

Symbols and abbreviations used in the text:

A   - Access/Mastercard/Eurocard
Ax - American Express
Dc - Diners Club
V   - Visa/Barclaycard

*S*ightseeing

London's history begins in AD43, when invading Romans bridged the Thames. Their London Wall determined the shape of what is still called the City of London. After the devastation of three-fifths of the City during the Great Fire of 1666, a massive scheme grew out of the ashes and extended beyond the City, creating the London we know today. Central districts of the capital take their names from villages which were absorbed into the great plan.
London has, naturally, changed enormously through the years, but every stage of its history can be traced through the buildings, monuments, churches and famous houses.

SIGHTS

Albert Memorial   91 F4
Kensington Gore SW7. Due to extensive restoration work this impressive Gothic memorial is currently covered. A Visitors' Centre houses an exhibition showing the extent and scope of the work. A tribute to Queen Victoria's consort, Prince Albert, it stands at 175ft (53m) with a 14ft (4m) statue of the Prince (by John Foley).

Bank of England   85 H4
Threadneedle St EC2. 0171-601 5545. Established 1694 and nicknamed 'The Old Lady of Threadneedle Street'. Serves as banker to the government, as well as leading British and international banks and acts as custodian of the nation's gold reserves. Outer walls still the original design of Sir John Soane (architect to the Bank 1788-1833); interior rebuilt by Sir Herbert Baker 1925. The Bank of England Museum is the only part *open to the public* (see page 17).

Banqueting House   95 F4
Whitehall SW1. 0171-930 4179. Inigo Jones 1619-25. The only surviving part of Whitehall Palace, used for state and court ceremonies. Its main feature is a magnificent ceiling painted by Rubens. Charles I was executed outside the Banqueting House having stepped through one of its high windows onto the scaffold. *Open 10.00-17.00 Mon-Sat.* Charge.

British Telecom Tower   82 A1
Howland St W1. Eric Bedford, 1964. Once the tallest building in London, and still commanding a prominent place on the skyline. 580ft (177m) topped by a 39ft (12m) mast

with radar aerial. Now houses telecommunications equipment and offices. *Not open to the public.*

Canary Wharf
An 80-acre (35ha) 'development' with shops, offices, apartments, restaurants, gardens and waterfront promenades. It is also home to the tallest building in the United Kingdom, Canary Wharf Tower, which stands 50 storeys high, at 800ft (244m), and dominates the skyline for miles around. *Tower not open to the public.*

The Cenotaph   95 E3
Whitehall SW1. Sir Edwin Lutyens (1920) – built to honour the dead of the First World War, it now commemorates those who died in both World Wars. The word comes from the Greek *kenos* meaning empty and *taphos* meaning tomb. The annual service of Remembrance takes place here at the eleventh hour on the nearest Sunday to the eleventh day of the eleventh month (see page 15).

Chelsea Royal Hospital   105 C5
Embankment SW3. 0171-730 0161. Established 1682 by Charles II for veteran soldiers. Designed by Wren and opened in 1689, admitting 476 army pensioners. Inside are fine carvings, panelling and several royal portraits. The Chelsea Flower Show is held annually in the grounds in May (see page 14). *Open 10.00-12.00 & 14.00-16.00 Mon-Sat, 14.00-16.00 Sun. Closed Sun Oct-Mar.* Free.

The City of London
A thriving financial and commercial centre which has within its 'square mile' such famous institutions as the Bank of England, the Stock Exchange, the Royal Courts of Justice and the Guildhall. Bustling by day with office workers, the area is almost deserted by night. Administered as a separate unit, the City has its own Lord Mayor and Corporation as well as its own police force. The high-rise buildings and modern offices stand out clearly but it is probably the magnificent dome of St Paul's Cathedral which dominates the City skyline.

Downing Street   95 E3
SW1. Built by Sir George Downing MP in the 17thC. Of the original houses, only Nos.10, 11 and 12 remain. No.10 is the official residence of the Prime Minister, No.11 that of the Chancellor of the Exchequer and No.12 is the Party Whips' Office. *Wrought-iron gates prevent direct public access.*

Royal Naval College, Greenwich

Greenwich *See also London's River pp29-35.*
Cutty Sark King William Walk SE10. 0181-858
3445. One of the great tea clippers, built 1869,
now in dry dock. Explore the galley and
cabins. Close by is *Gipsy Moth IV*, in which
Sir Francis Chichester sailed single-handed
round the world in 1966. Both *open Apr-
Sep 10.00-17.30 Mon-Sat, 12.00-18.00 Sun. Cutty
Sark* also *open Oct-Mar 10.00-17.00 Mon-Sat,
12.00-17.00 Sun.* Charge.
Old Royal Observatory Greenwich Park
SE10. 0181-858 4422. Part of the National
Maritime Museum and including Flamsteed
House. Founded by Charles II in 1675 and
designed by Wren. Stand astride the
Meridian line to be in both eastern and west-
ern hemispheres simultaneously. Extensive
collection of time-measuring instruments and
London's only camera obscura. Also houses
a planetarium. *Open 10.00-17.00 Mon-Sun.*
Charge.
Royal Naval College Greenwich SE10. 0181-
858 2154. On the site of the former Greenwich
Palace, Wren's beautiful baroque building
(1694) houses Sir James Thornhill's amazing
Painted Hall (which took nearly 20 years to

complete). The palace became Greenwich
Hospital in 1705, and later in 1873, a college
for the higher education of Naval Officers.
Open 14.30-17.00 Mon-Sun. Free.
Guildhall **83 G3**
off Gresham St EC2. 0171-606 3030. 1411-40
with alterations to the façade by George
Dance 1789 and later restorations 1953 by Sir
Giles Gilbert Scott. The Great Hall is used for
ceremonial occasions – there was a banquet
here to celebrate Queen Elizabeth II's coronation. Library established 1423 from money
left by Dick Whittington, London's most
famous Lord Mayor. Contains a fine collection of books, prints, maps and drawings.
The medieval crypt is the most extensive of
its kind in London. Great Hall *open 10.00-
17.00 Mon-Sat.* Free. Specialist library con-
cerned with the history of London *open
09.30-17.00 Mon-Sat.* Free.
Houses of Parliament **95 F4**
Westminster SW1. 0171-219 3000. Originally
the Palace of Westminster, and a principal
royal palace until 1512. Became known as
'parliament' or 'place to speak' in 1550.
Westminster Hall, one of the few remaining

Houses of Parliament

parts of the original royal palace, has an impressive hammerbeam roof. The present Victorian-Gothic building was designed 1847 by Sir Charles Barry and Augustus Pugin specifically to house Parliament and has 1100 rooms, 100 staircases and over 2 miles (3km) of passages. Cleaned in recent years to reveal their full architectural beauty, the Houses of Parliament and Big Ben – the bell clock housed in the adjoining St Stephen's Tower – make up London's most famous landmark. *To arrange a tour or to visit during Prime Minister's Question Time, contact your MP (or embassy for foreign visitors). For admission to debates, queue at St Stephen's entrance: 14.30-17.30 Mon, Tue & Thur, 10.00-14.30 Wed, 09.30-15.00 Fri. No small children. Free.*

Hyde Park Corner   93 F3

SW1. A toll gate at this spot originally marked London's western limits. In the centre is Constitution Arch, an Ionic Screen of three classical-style triumphal arches built in 1825 by Decimus Burton. Once intended as an imposing and pleasing feature of the journey from Buckingham Palace to Hyde Park, its attraction is somewhat marred by the heavy traffic which surrounds it.

Inns of Court

There are four great Inns of Court, dating from the 14thC, which act as a law school and have the exclusive privilege of calling candidates to the English Bar. Before they are eligible to be called, prospective barristers must pass the Bar exams, join one of the four Inns of Court and dine 24 times in the halls!

Gray's Inn   83 H1

Holborn WC1 (entrance from passage next to 22 High Holborn). 0171-405 8164. An Inn of Court since the 14thC, with a 16thC Hall restored after bomb damage. Francis Bacon had chambers here from 1577 until his death. He reportedly laid out the gardens and planted the Catalpa tree. Hall *open by written application to the Under Treasurer.* Gardens *open 12.00-14.30 Mon-Fri. Free.*

Lincoln's Inn   83 H3

WC2. 0171-405 1393. Parts of Lincoln's Inn date back to the 13thC and it still has a Dickensian atmosphere. Famous former members include Disraeli, Gladstone and Oliver Cromwell. *Open 10.00-16.00 Mon-Fri (gardens open 12.30-14.30 only). Admission to the chapel outside these hours and to the Hall and Library by written application to the Treasury Office, Whitehall SW1. Free.*

Inner Temple   84 A5

Crown Office Row EC4. 0171-797 8250. The Inner Temple dates from 1505. Prince Henry's Room, above the Gateway (1610), is the old-

Middle Temple

est domestic building in London and home to the Samuel Pepys Club and Pepysian memorabilia. *Open 10.00-16.00 Mon-Fri by arrangement. Closed Sat, Sun, Bank hols and legal vacations. Free.*

Middle Temple   84 A4

Middle Temple Lane EC4. 0171-353 4355. Dates from 1570. Together with the Inner Temple it comprises courtyards, alleys, gardens and warmly coloured brick buildings. *Open 10.00-12.00 & 14.00-16.00 Mon-Fri by arrangement. Closed Sat, Sun, Bank hols, Aug and during examinations. Free.*

Jewel Tower   95 E5

Old Palace Yard SW1. 0171-222 2219. 14thC surviving fragment of the old Palace of Westminster, once the safe for Edward III's jewels, clothes and furs, and now home to a collection of pottery and interesting objects found during excavations of the area. *Re-opens after refurbishment May 1996 Easter-Sep 10.00-13.00 & 14.00-18.00 Mon-Sun; Oct-Easter 10.00-13.00 & 14.00-16.00 Mon-Sun. Charge.*

Lambeth Palace   95 G6

Lambeth Palace Rd SE1. 0171-928 8282. Official London residence of the Archbishop of Canterbury since 1197. 13thC crypt and Tudor gatehouse, built by Archbishop Morton in 1486-1501. The gloves worn by Charles I when he went to the scaffold are on display and there is a brass plate commemorating the negligence of the gardener who stuck his fork through Archbishop Laud's tortoise. *Tours (very restricted) Wed or Thur by written application to the Booking Secretary. Charge.*

Law Courts   83 H4

Strand WC2. 0171-936 6000. Victorian-Gothic building housing the Royal Courts of Justice. Over 1000 rooms and 3½ miles of corridor. *Open to the public 10.00-16.30 Mon-Fri. Over 16s for criminal cases; over 14s for civil cases. Not in session Aug & Sep but still open. Free.*

Lloyds of London   **86 A4**
Lime St EC3. 0171-623 7100. Impressive glass
and aluminium structure, by the Richard
Rogers Partnership (also responsible for the
Pompidou Centre in Paris). Spectacular at
night, this multi-faceted, 12-storey, 6-towered
structure is the headquarters for the international insurance market. Huge dealing room
with a 246ft (75m) atrium housing the famous
Lutine Bell. *Not open to the public.*

London Wall
EC2. Surviving parts of the Roman and
medieval wall around the original City of
London can still be seen at St Alphage
Garden (**85 F2**) on the north side of London
Wall EC2; St Giles Churchyard, Cripplegate St
EC1 (**85 E1**); Jewry St EC3 (**86 C4**); off Trinity
Square EC3 (**86 B6**) and in the Tower of
London EC3 (**86 C6**).

Mansion House   **85 G4**
Walbrook EC4. 0171-626 2500. Residence of

Lloyds of London

Monument

the Lord Mayor of London, built 1739 by
George Dance the Elder. Palladian mansion
with several majestic rooms such as the Ball
Room, Banqueting Room and Egyptian Hall,
lavishly decorated in 23-carat gold. *Open to
parties of 15-40 people Tue-Thur by written
application.*

Marble Arch   **80 D5**
W1. John Nash 1827. Based on the Arch of
Constantine in Rome. Moved to its present
site on the north-east corner of Hyde Park in
1851. Only senior members of the Royal
Family and the King's Troop Royal Horse
Artillery may pass through it. This was once
the spot for the Tyburn Gallows, the main
execution site from the 14thC to 1783. Up to
21 victims a day were hanged here.

Monument   **85 H6**
Monument St EC3. 0171-626 2717. Wren 1671-7.
Built to commemorate the Great Fire of 1666
the Monument stands at 202ft (61m), one foot
in height for every foot in distance from
where the fire started in Pudding Lane. Its
summit is reached by 311 steps up a spiral
staircase, so beware if you are inclined to feel
dizzy. Magnificent views once you make it!
*Re-opens April 1996 after restoration. Phone
for details of opening times.* Charge.

NatWest Tower   **86 A3**
Bishopsgate EC2. This 600ft (183m) tower

Piccadilly Circus

(1980) was the tallest building in Britain until the Canary Wharf Tower was completed in 1991. It is a slender, shining structure with a curious, if appropriate, pin-striped effect due to the closeness of its vertical lines. Dominating the skyline in the City, it houses offices of the National Westminster Bank. *Not open to the public.*

Nelson's Column   **94 D1**
Trafalgar Sq WC2. William Railton 1839-42. 145ft (44m) granite column surmounted by a 16ft (5m) stone statue of Admiral Lord Nelson by E.H. Baily which was erected in 1843. The statue is missing his eye and arm, both lost in battle. Four lions surrounding the column were added 1868 by Landseer.

Old Bailey   **84 D3**
Old Bailey EC4. 0171-248 3277. Also known as the Central Criminal Court, the present building opened in 1907 on the site of Newgate Prison. It has been the scene for many famous trials – Oscar Wilde in 1895, Dr Crippen in 1910, J.R. Christie in 1953 and Peter Sutcliffe, 'the Yorkshire Ripper', in 1981. Public viewing gallery. *Open 10.30-13.00 & 14.00-16.00 Mon-Fri. Minimum age 14 (must be accompanied by an adult if under 16). Free.*

Pall Mall   **82 C1**
Pall Mall SW1. Early 19thC opulence. Gentlemen's clubs were established on this fine street as exclusive havens for their members. The Reform Club (No.104), by Sir Charles Barry, founded 1832, was where the fictitious character Phileas Fogg began his trip *Around the World in 80 Days*. The Travellers' Club (No.106) was founded in 1819 as a point of reunion for travellers. The Athenaeum (No.107) is the most elite, found-

ed for artists, writers and scientists and now the venue for high-powered conversation amongst ministers, bishops and academics.

Piccadilly Circus   **82 C6**
W1. The confluence of five major thoroughfares – Regent Street, Shaftesbury Avenue, Haymarket, Piccadilly and Lower Regent Street. Always busy, the name has become synonymous with anything overcrowded or chaotic! Fountain and statue of Eros by Gilbert (1893). The world-famous neon adver-

Nelson's Column

Royal Albert Hall

tising hoardings make it a far cry from its original elegant designs – the first, for Bovril and Schweppes at the turn of the century, caused a great scandal. The London Pavilion and Trocadero Centre provide one-stop shopping alongside entertainment and places to eat.

Regent Street   **82 A4**
W1. John Nash, asked by George IV (then Prince of Wales) to construct a link from Carlton House (now demolished) to the royal country home near Regent's Park, not only designed the route for Regent Street, but most of the buildings along it. This took many years since it was pieced together to conform with various architectural styles along the way. Initially acclaimed, its imminent destruction was celebrated in 1927 when George V and his Queen drove down its flower-decked length – it was then rebuilt from end to end.

Ritz Hotel   **94 A1**
Piccadilly W1. 0171-493 8181. Designed by the Swiss hotelier, César Ritz, it opened in May 1906. The archways fronting onto Piccadilly are based on the rue de Rivoli in Paris and the interior is in Louis XVI style. The restaurant has provided sustenance for, amongst others, Pavlova, Diaghilev and Caruso. The word 'ritzy' has become synonymous over the years with opulence, luxury and ostentation.

Royal Albert Hall   **91 G4**
Kensington Gore SW7. 0171-589 8212. After an idea by Prince Albert, it was originally built as the 'Hall of Arts & Sciences', and prefixed with 'Royal Albert' at the last minute by Queen Victoria. Oval, not circular as you might imagine, this is the venue for a wide variety of events from organ recitals to boxing matches. New home of the Royal Philharmonic Orchestra.

Royal Exchange   **85 H4**
Cnr Threadneedle St and Cornhill EC3. Present building (the third) 1844 by Sir William Tite. The original was destroyed in the Great Fire of London in 1666.

Smithfield   **84 D2**
EC1. Historical site of the murder of Wat Tyler, tournaments, public executions, cattle market and the famous Bartholomew Fair. Smithfield Market is the largest meat market in the world.

Soho   **82 C5**
An area bound by Regent Street, Oxford Street, Shaftesbury Avenue and Charing Cross Road. Lively, safe area; only a handful of peep shows and strip joints survive from its seedier days. Narrow 18thC and 19thC streets full of fascinating foreign food shops, restaurants, street markets, flashing neon and nightlife of all sorts. Chinatown radiates from Gerrard Street.

Spitalfields   **86 C1**
E1. The centre of silk-weaving in England was established by the influx of Flemish and French weavers in the 16thC and 17thC. The

industry reached its height at the end of the 18thC and early 19thC when about 17,000 looms were in use and a large area of East London was dependent on these family concerns. Fournier Street (**86 D1**) has some good examples of Dutch-style houses of the time. The industry collapsed some 100 years ago, but the streets here are still steeped in history and tradition.

Tower Bridge   **98 C2**
This spectacular Victorian-Gothic structure bridge was opened in 1894 and is one of the world's best-known double-bascule bridges, which still opens to allow tall ships to pass through. There are wonderful views from the walkway and a fascinating museum within the towers which details the history, design and operation of this famous Thames landmark. (See page 20).

Tower of London   **86 C6**
Tower Hill EC3. 0171-709 0765. A keep, a prison and still a fortress, the Tower has served as a palace, a place of execution, and in its time has housed the Royal Mint, the Royal Observatory, the Royal Menagerie, and the Public Records. Now famous for the Bloody Tower, Traitors' Gate, the ravens, the Crown Jewels, the Armouries and the Yeomen Warders (or Beefeaters). British monarchs imprisoned here include Edward III, Henry VII and Elizabeth I, kept prisoner by her sister Queen Mary when she refused to convert to Roman Catholicism. Other prisoners have included Sir Thomas More, Guy Fawkes and his fellow plotters, Sir Walter Ralegh, and, more recently, Rudolf Hess, detained during the Second World War. Also the site of many executions including two of Henry VIII's six wives – Anne Boleyn in 1536, and Catherine Howard in 1542 – both of whom were given the privilege of a quiet execution on Tower Green. The state of the art Jewel House contains the Crown Jewels, with which the new monarch is invested at the coronation ceremony. These include the Star of Africa, the biggest cut diamond in the world. *Open Mar-Oct 09.00-18.00 Mon-Sat, 10.00-18.00 Sun; Nov-Feb 09.00-17.00 Mon-Sat, 10.00-17.00 Sun. Be prepared for long queues in summer.* Charge.

Trafalgar Square   **94 D1**
WC2. Laid out by Sir Charles Barry 1829. Nelson's column (see page 7) stands in the middle. Fountains by Lutyens. Famous for political rallies, pigeons and the New Year's Eve revellers.

Whitehall   **95 E2**
Wide thoroughfare, once part of the main route linking Westminster to the City. Now used for ceremonial and state processions, it is lined with Government offices including the Old Admiralty, Old Scotland Yard, the Foreign Office, the Commonwealth Office, the Treasury and the War Office.

PLACES OF WORSHIP

Entry to all churches and cathedrals is *free* unless otherwise stated.

All-Hallows-by-the-Tower   **86 B6**
Byward St EC3. 0171-481 2928. From here Samuel Pepys viewed the devastation after the Great Fire of London. The altarpiece of the *Last Supper* is by Brian Thomas. Crypt Museum with Roman pavement and brass rubbing. Church *open 09.00-18.00 Mon-Fri, 10.00-17.00 Sat & Sun.* Free. Crypt *open 10.00-16.30 Mon-Fri, 11.00-16.00 Sat, 13.00-16.00 Sun.* Charge.

All Souls, Langham Place   **81 H2**
Langham Place W1. 0171-580 3522. Nash's only church, built as part of his scheme for Regent Street and Regent's Park, completed 1824. Unusual Corinthian columns combined with a needle spire.

Bevis Marks Synagogue   **86 B4**
Heneage La (off Bevis Marks) EC3. 0171-626 1274. Avis 1701. Britain's oldest surviving synagogue with fine windows and brass chandeliers from Amsterdam.

Brompton Oratory   **92 A6**
Brompton Rd SW7. 0171-589 4811. Herbert Gribble 1884. Baroque style, based on the Chiesa Nuova in Rome and the centre of Roman Catholicism in London until Westminster Cathedral was completed in 1903. Ornate interior and fine statues, some of them originals from the Cathedral of Siena.

Chelsea Old Church, All Saints   **102 C6**
Chelsea Embankment SW3. 0171-352 5627. Henry VIII and Jane Seymour married here privately before their state wedding in 1536. Original church dates from 1157, but has been substantially added to since. South chapel rebuilt by Sir Thomas More who wished to be buried here but his head was taken to Canterbury after his execution. The church was severely bombed in 1941 and restored by Walter Godfrey.

Christ Church Spitalfields   **86 D2**
Commercial St E1. 0171-247 7202. One of Hawksmoor's finest churches (1720), with an unusual tower and octagonal spire. In the 18thC Huguenot refugees worked the fields of Spital nearby, which accounts for many of the gravestones from this time bearing French names. The church was partly restored in the late 19thC.

London Central Mosque

cabinets in the crypt museum are dedicated by Sir Max Aitken to his father, Lord Beaverbrook (one-time owner of the *Daily Express* newspaper).

St Clement Danes   **83 F6**
Strand WC2. 0171-242 8282. First built 9thC, rebuilt by Wren 1681. Destroyed by bombing in 1941, restored and rededicated in 1958, it now serves as the central church of the Royal Air Force. On occasions the bells ring 'Oranges and Lemons', made famous in the nursery rhyme of the same name.

St Giles Cripplegate   **85 F2**
Fore St EC2. 0171-606 3630. 12thC, rebuilt 1537, and restored by Godfrey Allen in 1952 after bombing. Oliver Cromwell married Elizabeth Bourchier here in 1620 and Milton was buried here in 1674. Some of the remains of the London Wall are in the churchyard.

St John Smith Square   **95 E6**
Smith Sq SW1. 0171-222 1061. Nicknamed 'Queen Anne's Footstool'. Archer 1721-8. Destroyed by fire in 1742. Interior redesigned, only to be blitzed in 1941. Since then it has been restored to Archer's original design by a charitable trust and is now used mainly as a concert hall.

St Margaret Westminster   **95 E4**
Parliament Sq SW1. 0171-222 6382. Rebuilt 1486-1523 and again after repeated damage in World War II. Splendid early 16thC east window and exquisite stained glass. Parish church of the House of Commons since 1614 and the site of many distinguished weddings and burials. Samuel Pepys was married here in 1655, as were John Milton in 1656 and Winston Churchill in 1908. William Caxton, Sir Walter Ralegh and Admiral Blake are buried here.

St Martin-in-the-Fields   **94 D1**
Trafalgar Sq WC2. 0171-930 1862. Founded in the 12thC and rebuilt many times. Present construction by James Gibbs 1722-4 with a famous spire and portico. In 1924, Dick Sheppard, the vicar, conducted the first radio broadcast service from the church. Many notable events have taken place here – Charles II christened 1630, funerals of Nell Gwynne, Hogarth, and Sir Joshua Reynolds. Crypt *open 10.00-20.00 Mon-Sat, 12.00-18.00 Sun*; bookshop *10.00-19.30 Mon-Sat, 12.00-18.00 Sun*; brass rubbing centre *10.00-18.00 Mon-Sat, 12.00-18.00 Sun* (charge); café *10.00-20.00 Mon-Sat, 12.00-18.00 Sun;* craft market and gallery *12.00-18.00 Mon-Sun.*

St Mary-le-Bow   **85 E4**
Cheapside EC2. 0171-248 5139. During the 14thC the curfew was rung on its famous bells, which is probably the origin of the idea

London Central Mosque   **70 B4**
146 Park Rd NW8. 0171-724 3363. Graceful building on the edge of Regent's Park, completed 1978. The religious centre for London's Muslim community with a 75ft (25m) golden dome and a rich interior – marble floors from Algeria, tiles from Turkey, Iranian carpets and Jordanian chandeliers.

St Bartholomew-the-Great   **84 C2**
West Smithfield EC1. 0171-606 5171. Oldest church in London and the only surviving part of an Augustinian priory founded 1123. Unusual oriel window and the only pre-Reformation font in the City. The tomb of its founder, Rahere, Henry I's court jester, and later founder of St Bartholomew's Hospital, is to be found here, amongst other fine monuments. Hogarth was christened here in 1697.

St Bride's   **84 B4**
Fleet St EC4. 0171-353 1301. Discoveries made by archaeologists after St Bride's was bombed in 1940 show that St Bridget founded the first Christian church here in the 6thC. Wynkyn de Worde, Caxton's apprentice, brought the printing press to Fleet Street and was buried at St Bride's in 1535. Associations with the press continue to this day – display

St Martin-in-the-Fields

that to be a true Cockney you have to be born within the sound of 'Bow Bells'. Destroyed in the Great Fire, rebuilt by Wren 1670-83 and restored again by Laurence King 1956-62. Superb steeple, one of Wren's finest, stands at 217ft (66m).

St Paul's Cathedral   **85 F4**
Ludgate Hill EC4. 0171-248 4619/2705. Wren's masterpiece is the fifth cathedral on this site, the first was founded in AD604 by St Ethelbert of Kent, first Christian king in England. The Whispering Gallery in the dome is particularly impressive – the slightest sound carries from one side to the other, 107ft (33m) away. Grinling Gibbons' choir stalls and organ, which has been played by Handel and Mendelssohn, are magnificent. Nelson and Wellington are among the famous buried here and the Prince and Princess of Wales were married here in 1981.

St Peter-ad-Vincula   **86 C6**
Tower of London, Tower Hill EC3. 0171-709 0765. Much restored church built c1512 for use by prisoners in the Tower. Full of royal and noble bones including Anne Boleyn, Thomas Cromwell, Catherine Howard, Sir Thomas More, Lady Jane Grey and her husband Lord Guildford Dudley.

Southwark Cathedral   **97 G1**
Borough High St SE1. 0171-407 3708. Founded

in the 7thC. Work began on the present cathedral in 1220, making it the earliest of London's Gothic churches. Left to decay significantly during Elizabeth I's reign and leased as pig sties, it was repaired in the early 19thC by George Gwilt the Younger. Tower dates from 1520 and the nave from 1894-7. Magnificent collection of monuments. Chapter House includes a restaurant *open 08.30-18.00 Mon-Fri.*

Temple Church   **84 A5**
Inner Temple La EC4. 0171-353 1736. One of only four remaining early Gothic round churches built by the Knight Templars, 12thC-13thC.

Westminster Abbey   **95 E5**
Broad Sanctuary SW1. 0171-222 5152. Original church founded by Edward the Confessor 1065. His tomb lies behind the high altar. Rebuilding commenced 1245 by Henry III and was largely completed by 1506, although the West Towers (started by Wren) were not finished until 1734 by Hawksmoor. On Christmas Day 1066 William I was crowned here – since then the Abbey has traditionally been the coronation church of the new monarch. Many royal and historical figures are buried here. The Tomb of the Unknown Warrior in the nave represents the thousands who died in World War I. Poets' Corner is the

St Paul's Cathedral

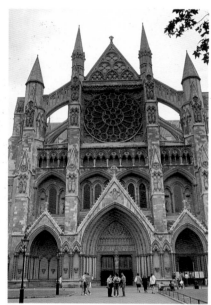
Westminster Abbey

final resting place of Dryden, Browning, Sheridan and Tennyson. Notice the glorious sculpted angels in the south transept and fine tiled floor of the Chapter House. *Restoration nearly complete at time of publication.*

Westminster RC Cathedral   **94 A6**
Ashley Place SW1. 0171-834 7452. The headquarters of the Catholic Church in Britain. Completed 1903 in Byzantine style, with glorious marble mosaics and the widest nave in England.

STATUES

Achilles   **93 F2**
Park Lane W1. A 20ft (6.5m) bronze by Westmacott 1822.

Alfred the Great   **97 F5**
Trinity Church Sq SE1. Unknown origins, but undoubtedly the oldest statue in London, dating back to the 14thC.

Boadicea (Boudicca)   **95 F4**
Westminster Bridge SW1. Thornycroft. Unveiled 1902, depicts the British queen riding with her daughters in a chariot.

Sir Charles Chaplin   **82 D6**
Leicester Sq WC2. John Doubleday. With customary bowler hat and walking stick. Unveiled 1981 by the actor Sir Ralph Richardson.

Charles I   **94 D1**
Trafalgar Sq SW1. Hubert le Sueur, erected 1675 after the Restoration. The Royal Stuart Society lays a wreath here every year on the anniversary of his execution, 30 January.

Sir Winston Churchill   **95 E4**
Parliament Sq SW1. 1973 Ivor Roberts-Jones. Magnificent bronze of one of Britain's greatest statesmen, in naval overcoat.

Oliver Cromwell   **95 E5**
Old Palace Yard SW1. Bronze by Sir Hamo Thornycroft (1899). Significantly he stands with his back to the Houses of Parliament!

Elizabeth I   **84 B4**
St Dunstan-in-the-West, Fleet St EC4. Cast during the queen's lifetime, in 1586, by William Kerwin.

Eros   **82 C6**
Piccadilly Circus W1. Alfred Gilbert 1893. Officially represents the Angel of Christian Charity – restored 1984.

Peter Pan   **91 G1**
Kensington Gardens W2. By Frampton 1912. Delightful figure erected overnight as a surprise for the children. Much of the carving of the animals at its base has been worn away over the years by children's stroking hands.

Captain Scott   **94 C1**
Waterloo Place SW1. Bronze of her husband in full arctic kit by Lady Scott, erected in 1915.

Sir Charles Chaplin

Sir Winston Churchill

Elizabeth I

Peter Pan

Victoria Memorial   **94 A4**
Before Buckingham Palace SW1. By Brock 1911, impressive memorial to Queen Victoria, which includes a fine, dignified statue of the queen, the best of many.

Duke of Wellington   **93 B1**
Hyde Park Corner SW1. Huge bronze by J.E. Boehm (1888) of the Duke astride his favourite horse, Copenhagen, and looking towards Apsley House (see page 21) where he lived.

BLUE PLAQUES

Since 1866, blue plaques have been used to mark houses and other buildings associated with famous people or events, commemorating the lives of architects, artists, composers, politicians, scientists, soldiers and writers.

Baden-Powell, Robert Stephenson   **91 F4**
Founder of the Boy Scout movement. Lived at 9 Hyde Park Gate SW7.

Bligh, William   **97 A6**
Commander of HMS *Bounty*. Lived at 100 Lambeth Rd SE1.

Chaplin, Sir Charles Spencer   **97 A5**
Actor and comedian. Lived at 287 Kennington Rd SE11.

Churchill, Sir Winston Leonard Spencer
Prime Minister 1940-45 and 1951-55. Lived at 34 Eccleston Sq SW1 (**103 H2**) and died at 28 Hyde Park Gate SW7 (**91 F4**).

Darwin, Charles   **73 C6**
Naturalist. Lived on the site of 110 Gower St WC1 (now part of University College, London).

De Gaulle, General Charles   **95 C2**
André Joseph Marie
De Gaulle set up the HQ of the Free French Forces at 4 Carlton Gardens SW1.

Dickens, Charles   **73 H6**
Author. Lived at 48 Doughty St WC1 (*open to the public,* see page 22), and at Tavistock House, Tavistock Sq WC1 (**73 D5**).

Fleming, Sir Alexander   **101 H6**
Scientist, discoverer of penicillin. Lived at 20a Danvers St SW3.

Handel, George Frederick   **81 G5**
Composer and musician. Lived and died at 25 Brook St W1.

Hardy, Thomas   **83 F6**
Poet and novelist. Lived at Adelphi Terrace WC2 and at 172 Trinity Rd, Tooting SW17.

Johnson, Dr Samuel
Poet and lexicographer. Lived at 17 Gough Sq EC4 (**84 B3**) and died at Johnson's Court, Fleet St EC4 (**74 B4**).

Kennedy, John Fitzgerald   **91 H4**
President of the USA 1961-63. Lived at 14 Prince's Gate SW7.

Kipling, Rudyard   **95 F1**
Poet and story writer. Lived at 43 Villiers St WC2.

Lawrence, David Herbert
Novelist and poet. Lived at 1 Byron Villas, Vale of Health NW3.

Lawrence, Thomas Edward   **95 E5**
('Lawrence of Arabia')
Soldier and adviser on Arab affairs during
World War 1. Lived at 14 Barton St SW1.

Marx, Karl Heinrich   **82 C3**
Communist and author. Lived at 28 Dean St
W1, above the Italian restaurant Leoni's Quo
Vadis.

Mozart, Wolfgang Amadeus   **103 F2**
Composer and musician. Composed his first
symphony at 180 Ebury St SW1.

Napoleon III (Charles Louis   **94 B2**
Napoleon Bonaparte)
Emperor of France. Lived at 1c King St SW1.

Nelson, Lord Horatio   **81 G4**
Naval hero. Lived on the site of 147 New
Bond St W1 and at 103 New Bond St W1.

Nightingale, Florence   **93 F1**
Nursing pioneer. Lived and died on the site of
10 South St W1.

Orwell, George (Eric Arthur Blair)   **66 A2**
Novelist and essayist. Lived at 50 Lawford Rd
NW5 and at 27b Canonbury Sq N1.

Pepys, Samuel
Diarist. Born in a house on the site of
Westminster Bank, Salisbury Court EC4
(**84 B4**). Lived at 12 Buckingham St WC2
(**83 F6**).

Turner, Joseph Mallord William
Painter. Lived at 23 Queen Anne St W1 (**81 G3**)
and at 119 Cheyne Walk SW3 (**102 B6**).

Whittington, Richard (Dick)   **85 F5**
English merchant and four times Lord Mayor
of London. Lived at a house on the site of 20
College Hill EC4. Buried at St Michael Royal
Church, College Hill EC4 (**85 F5**).

Wren, Sir Christopher   **85 E6**
Architect. Lived at 49 Bankside SE1 during
the building of St Paul's Cathedral.

ANNUAL EVENTS

For exact dates, times and places, where not
given, contact one of the Tourist Information
Centres (see page 59).

JANUARY/FEBRUARY/MARCH

Lord Mayor of Westminster's   **92 C1**
New Year's Day Parade
Information: 0181-566 8586. Marching bands,
colourful floats and veteran vehicles. Starts
Piccadilly and ends in Hyde Park where the
entertainment continues. *1 Jan.* Free.

International Boat Show   **100 A5**
Earl's Court Exhibition Centre, Warwick Rd
SW5. 0171-385 1200. The latest pleasure
crafts, yachts and equipment to marvel at.
Early Jan. Charge.

Chinese New Year Festival   **82 D5**
Chinatown, Gerrard St W1. Noisy, colourful
affair celebrating Chinese New Year. Papier-
mâché dragons, extravagant costumes and
brightly-lit festivities. *Jan or Feb.* Free.

Oxford v. Cambridge Boat Race
River Thames, Putney SW15 to Mortlake
SW14. The annual rowing challenge between
the dark and light blues (Oxford and
Cambridge universities) has been taking
place since 1845. Plenty of vantage points
from bridges, banks or riverside pubs – get
there early for a good view. *Sat afternoon in
Mar or Apr.* Free.

APRIL/MAY/JUNE

Easter Show   **103 F6**
Battersea Park SW11. Colourful carnival –
funfair, side shows and various other enter-
tainments. *Easter Sun.* Charge

London Marathon
Information: 0171-620 4117. The world's
largest road race with a wide variety of com-
petitors from international marathon runners
to fancy dress charity runners. Starts
Greenwich Park SE10 and finishes
Westminster Bridge SW1 (**95 F4**). *Late Apr.*
Free to spectators.

Chelsea Flower Show   **102 D4**
Chelsea Royal Hospital, Royal Hospital Rd
SW3. 0171-834 4333. Superb floral displays
burst into bloom in the grounds of the Royal
Hospital. Exhibitions include extravagant
landscaped gardens, fruit and vegetable displays, garden equipment and other green-
fingered accessories. *For four days, third week
of May.* Charge.

Beating Retreat   **94 D3**
Horse Guards' Parade SW1. 0171-839 5323.
Colourful military display of marching and
drilling bands. Evening floodlit performances.
For tickets phone 0171-930 0292. Early Jun.
Charge.

Election of the Sheriffs of the   **85 G3**
City of London
Guildhall EC2. 0171-606 3030. Lord Mayor and
Aldermen of the City of London take part in a
colourful ceremony. *Midsummer's Day, unless
it falls on a Sat or Sun.* Free.

Lord's Test Match   **69 H3**
Lord's Cricket Ground, St John's Wood Rd

NW8. Ring 0171-289 8979 for tickets; 0171-286 8011 for information. A major ground for the British institution of cricket. The Test Match is over *five days Jun or Jul.* Charge.

**Royal Academy Summer Art   82 A6
Exhibition**

Royal Academy, Burlington House, Piccadilly W1. 0171-439 7438. Aspiring Cézannes and Hockneys enter their works to be admired and hopefully bought! Huge mixture of styles from amateur-looking oils to beautifully-crafted architectural designs. Be prepared for long queues. *Jun-mid Aug.* Charge.

Trooping the Colour   94 D3

Colourful pageant and procession to celebrate the Queen's official birthday. Royal party leaves Buckingham Palace at around *10.30* and proceeds along the Mall to Horse Guards' Parade then to Whitehall and back again. *11.00, Sat nearest 11 Jun.* Charge.

Wimbledon Lawn Tennis Championships

Church Rd SW19. Recorded information: 0181-946 2244. Height of the tennis circuit tournaments, and one of the most famous championships in the world. Early evening is the best time to go to avoid the crowds. *Tickets for Centre Court, No.1 and No.2 Court are awarded by public ballot, but you can queue for tickets for the other courts on the day of play. Last week Jun & first week Jul.* Charge.

JULY/AUGUST/SEPTEMBER

Henley Royal Regatta

Henley-on-Thames, Oxon. (01491) 572153. Smart outfits and even smarter picnics try to outdo each other on the bank while the skilled rowers do their stuff. *For exact dates phone the above number. Early Jul.* Free in public areas.

**Proms (Henry Wood Promenade   91 G4
Concerts)**

Royal Albert Hall, Kensington Gore SW7. 0171-589 8212. Classical music festival culminating in the famous Last Night of the Proms at the Royal Albert Hall. *Late Jul until Sep.* Charge.

Notting Hill Carnival   77 G6

Ladbroke Grove and Notting Hill W11. Started originally as a celebration of West Indian culture. A lively, noisy, colourful event with music, dancing in the streets and processions. *Sun* is children's day, and the main processions take place *Bank Holiday Monday. Last Mon in Aug.* Free.

OCTOBER/NOVEMBER/DECEMBER

Horse of the Year Show

Wembley Arena, Wembley, Middx. 0181-902 8833. Fine showjumping with many of the

world-famous competitors under one roof. *Early Oct.* Charge.

Christmas Lights   82 A5

Oxford St and Regent St W1. Bright and imaginative illuminations line the streets and shop windows to celebrate the season. Ceremoniously switched on in *Nov.* Free.

State Opening of Parliament   94 A4

The Queen goes from Buckingham Palace to the House of Lords to open Parliament after the summer recess. Good views from the north side of The Mall – get there early. *10.30 1st week Nov.* Free.

Lord Mayor's Procession & Show   85 G3

The newly-elected Lord Mayor is driven in the 1756 State Coach – with a procession of about 140 floats – from the Guildhall to the Law Courts to be received and sworn in by the Lord Chief Justice. Biggest ceremonial event in the City. *11.00 second Sat in Nov.* Free.

Remembrance Sunday   95 E3

The Cenotaph, Whitehall SW1. Service attended by the Queen and the Prime Minister to honour the dead of both World Wars. Takes place at the eleventh hour of the nearest Sunday to the eleventh day of the eleventh month – the anniversary of the armistice of World War I. Poppies sold in the street to raise money for ex-servicemen. Get there early for a good view. *11.00, Sun nearest 11 Nov.* Free.

Carol Services   95 E5

Westminster Abbey, Broad Sanctuary SW1. 0171-222 7110. Carol services on *26, 27 & 28 Dec.* Free.

Carol Singing   94 D1

Trafalgar Sq WC2. Carols are recorded on tape so you can just listen or sing along! *All through Dec.* Free.

New Year's Eve   94 D1

Trafalgar Sq WC2. Thousands gather in the square to bring in the New Year with massed singing of *Auld Lang Syne* and dancing round the fountains. Listen out for Big Ben tolling midnight. *31 Dec.* Free.

SIGHTSEEING TOURS

BY COACH

Big Bus Company

Waterside Way SW17. 0181-944 7810. Open-top double-decker bus tours with live commentary by London Tourist Board approved guides. *90-minute* tours and Stopper Tours depart *every ½ hour Mon-Fri, every 15 mins Sat, Sun & Bank hols. Phone for details of pick-up points.*

Evan Evans   **81 F3**
136 Wigmore St W1. 0171-930 2377. A well-established tour company which operates a variety of tours; *full day, morning* or *afternoon* plus a *2¹/₂-hr* general drive around the capital and a *30-minute* cruise on the Thames.

Harrods   **92 C5**
Sightseeing   Tours   Dept,   Harrods, Knightsbridge SW1. 0171-730 1234. The most luxurious coach tour of London, takes *2 hrs.* Taped commentary in eight different languages with refreshments on board.

Original London Sightseeing Tours
London Coaches, Jew's Row, Wandsworth SW18. 0181-877 1722. Round London tours in traditional double-decker buses, some of which are open-topped. A great favourite with children.

Star Safari
Full day and afternoon tours showing the lifestyles of the rich and famous with commentary by guides who will give you an insight into London and its glitterati. Tours depart from the Forum Hotel SW7 (**101 E1**), Victoria Station Tourist Information Centre SW1 (**103 H1**) and the Strand WC2 (**83 F6**). Bookings on (01932) 854721.

BY HORSE & CARRIAGE

The London Omnibus Company
Pick-up outside the London Transport Museum, Covent Garden WC2 (**83 F5**). They do *15-minute circuits* of Covent Garden *11.30 to lunchtime,* and *40-minute tours* of Trafalgar Square, Whitehall, Parliament Square and Westminster *afternoons to 15.30. Phone (01372) 727153 to book.*

WALKS

London Silver Jubilee Walkway
This 12-mile (19km) walkway was created for the Queen's Silver Jubilee in 1977. It circles the centre of London, passing close to many famous and historic buildings. The route starts at Leicester Square (**82 D5**) and is marked by steel discs set in the pavement . A leaflet is available from the London Tourist Board and Convention Bureau, Victoria Station Forecourt SW1 (**93 H6**).

CANAL TRIPS

Canal Waterbus   **79 E1**
London Waterbus Company, Camden Lock Place NW1. 0171-482 2550. Boats leave from Little Venice, stopping at London Zoo and continuing to Camden Lock *Apr-Sep 10.00-17.00 Mon-Sun; Oct 10.30-15.45 Mon-Sun; Nov-Mar 10.30-15.45 Sat & Sun.* Also run Limehouse/River Lea trips which explore the architecture and industrial history of London's quiet canalways *May-Oct 09.30-18.00 some Sats.*

Jason's Trip   **78 D1**
Opposite 60 Blomfield Rd W9. 0171-286 3428. The traditional narrowboat *Jason* leaves Little Venice for *1¹/₂-hr* return trip with commentary, through Regent's Park and via London Zoo to Camden Lock. Disembark to explore Camden Market. Refreshments available on board. *Phone for details of departure times.*

Jenny Wren Cruises
250 Camden High St NW1. 0171-485 4433. *Jenny Wren,* a traditional canal boat, gives a *1¹/₂-hr* round trip along Regent's Canal passing London Zoo, Regent's Park and Little Venice, with commentary on the canal and its history. From Camden Lock *Feb-Nov four times a day Mon-Sun.* They also run *My Fair Lady,* for evening supper cruises *20.00-23.00 Tue-Sat* and *Sunday lunchtime* cruises *13.00-15.30.*

The City with the dome of St Paul's Cathedral and the NatWest Tower

Museums & Galleries

It has long been a tradition that national museums and galleries were *free*, but many have now found it necessary to introduce either *voluntary contributions* or a fixed *admission fee*. Special exhibitions usually incur an *entrance fee*.

MUSEUMS

Alexander Fleming Laboratory Museum   **79 H3**

St Mary's Hospital, Praed St W2. 0171-725 6528. A reconstruction of the 1920s laboratory where penicillin was discovered. Guided tours are given by veterans of the antibiotic's introduction into medical practice, when it was hailed as a 'wonder drug'. *Open 10.00-13.00 Mon-Thur (by appointment afternoons), 10.00-17.00 Fri.* Charge.

Bank of England Museum   **85 H4**

Bank of England, Threadneedle St EC2. 0171-601 5545. Charts the Bank's history from 1694 to the high-tech world of modern banking. Houses unique English banknotes, gold bars and the Bank's silver collection. Shop. *Open Easter-Sep 10.00-17.00 Mon-Fri.* Free.

British Museum   **82 D2**

Great Russell St WC1. 0171-636 1555. The greatest collection of antiquities from all over the world, and the national collection of archaeology and ethnography with objects ranging from pre-historic to modern. The free information map at the entrance will help you plan your way around. Highlights include the Rosetta Stone (Room 25); Roman pavements (Room 16); the Elgin marbles (Room 8); 'Pete Marsh', the 2000-year-old murdered Lindow man found preserved in a Cheshire bog (Room 37); and the Sutton Hoo treasures from the burial site of a 7thC Anglo-Saxon king (Room 41). Also famous for mummies (Room 60). The domed Reading Room is where Karl Marx studied and wrote *Das Kapital (open to members only or on a guided tour).* Next to the main hall is the **British Library** which contains, by law, one copy of every book, periodical or newspaper printed in Great Britain. Collection includes two of the four *Magna Cartas* (Room 30), the *Lindisfarne Gospels* (Room 30a) and Shakespeare's first folio. Restaurant. Café. Excellent shop. Ask at the information desk for details of *guided tours lasting 1½ hrs.* Museum *open 10.00-17.00 Mon-Sat, 14.30-18.00 Sun.* Free (charge for special exhibitions and guided tours).

British Museum

Cabinet War Rooms   **94 D3**
Clive Steps, King Charles St SW1. 0171-930 6961. Intriguing underground suite of 21 rooms used by Winston Churchill and his War Cabinet from August 1939-September 1945 as a meeting, planning and information centre. See Churchill's bedroom, the desk from which he made some of his famous war-time broadcasts, and the original hot-line, the first telephone line with a scrambler used by Churchill to communicate with President Roosevelt. Shop. *Open 10.00-18.00 Mon-Sun (last admission 17.15).* Charge.

Clink Prison   **97 G1**
1 Clink Street SE1. 0171-403 6515. This exhibition, in the dark cellars of an old warehouse in Southwark, tells the strange story of the Clink prison and the Liberty of the Clink. Medieval punishments and prostitution as well. The more explicit material is displayed in an adults-only room – complete with red lights. Shop. *Open 10.00-18.00 Mon-Sun.* Charge.

Commonwealth Institute   **90 A5**
230 Kensington High St W8. 0171-603 4535. A modern building like a great glass tent. Discover the history, landscapes, wildlife and crafts of the Commonwealth on three floors of magical galleries which have continuous and changing exhibitions on every Commonwealth country, associated state and dependency. There are also cultural events and exhibitions. Reference library and shop. *Open 10.00-17.00 Mon-Sat, 14.00-17.00 Sun (closed Bank hols).* Charge.

Design Museum   **98 D3**
Butler's Wharf, Shad Thames SE1. 0171-403 6933. Recorded information 0171-378 6055. Founded by Sir Terence Conran, the aim is to make everyone aware of design – past, present and future – through a number of provocative exhibits. Furniture, gadgets and graphics from cars to tea-pots. Blueprint Café renowned for good food. Bookshop, library. *Open 11.30-18.00 Mon-Fri, 12.00-18.00 Sun.* Charge.

Geffrye Museum
Kingsland Rd, Hackney E2. 0171-739 9893. Housed in several early 18thC almshouses, exhibitions of the British living room from Tudor times to the 1950s including the prefabs of the 1940s, a panelled Elizabethan Room, an early Georgian Room and two stylish 1930s rooms. Café. Shop. Gardens. *Open 10.00-17.00 Tue-Sat, 14.00-17.00 Sun.* Free.

HMS *Belfast*   **98 A1**
Morgan's Lane, Tooley St SE1. 0171-407 6434. The last survivor of the Royal Navy's Second World War cruisers, now a permanent museum showing its role during wartime. Film shows and lectures. Shop. Café. *Open Apr-Sep 10.00-18.00 Mon-Sun; Oct-Mar 10.00-16.30 Mon-Sun. Last ticket 45 mins before closing.* Charge.

Imperial War Museum   **96 B6**
Lambeth Rd SE1. 0171-416 5000. Popular museum concentrating equally on the human as well as the mechanical side of war. Vast collection of tanks, weapons and aircraft including a Mark I Spitfire. 'The Blitz Experience' lets you see, feel and hear what it was like to be in London during the bombing of the 1940s. 'Operation Jericho' is a flight simulator allowing you to experience what it was like to fly with the RAF to release captured Resistance fighters. Good café. Shop. *Open 10.00-18.00 Mon-Sun.* Charge.

London Dungeon   **97 H1**
34 Tooley St SE1. 0171-403 0606. Set in dark vaults beneath London Bridge station, London Dungeon gruesomely recreates the horrors of sacrifice, torture, plague, murder and execution. Sophisticated technology, sound effects and dramatic lighting help bring to life a series of scenes involving real historical characters, from kings and queens to religious martyrs and common criminals. Special areas feature the Great Fire of London in 1666 and the guillotine of the French Revolution. Children under 10 must be accompanied by an adult. Shop. Restaurant. *Open 10.00-17.30 Mon-Sun (to 16.30 Oct-Mar).* Charge.

London Planetarium   **71 E6**
Marylebone Rd NW1. 0171-486 1121. Mind-boggling journey amongst the stars, space and the cosmos! Thousands of projected images become clear with an expert guide to explain the astronomical mysteries. The most advanced star projector in the world is used for the main show. Shop. Café. Shows *every 40 minutes Mon-Sun. First show 12.20 (10.20 Sat & Sun); last show 17.00.* Charge (combined entrance ticket with Madame Tussaud's available).

London Toy & Model Museum   **79 F5**
21-23 Craven Hill W2. 0171-706 8000. Vast collection of dolls, model cars, tin soldiers and countless other toys, spanning over 100 years. Miniature working railways, a 90-year-old model coal mine, an interactive airport control room, and in the garden a ride-on train. Shop. Café. *Open 10.00-17.30 Mon-Sun.* Charge.

London Transport Museum   **83 F5**
The Piazza, Covent Garden WC2. 0171-379 6344. The history of London's passenger transport system told through moving and static exhibits and audio-visual displays.

'Drive' modern-day tubes and buses and work the points and signals in a section of tunnel. Gallery houses London Transport's poster collection. Shop. *Open 10.00-18.00 Mon-Sun (last admission 17.15).* Charge.

Madame Tussaud's   **71 E6**

Marylebone Rd NW1. 0171-935 6861. Amongst the waxwork effigies of the famous and notorious meet the Royal Family, Pavarotti, Nelson Mandela and Cher. Murderers lurk in the Chamber of Horrors, which harbours evil-looking villains and stories of murder most foul. Enjoy the sights and sounds of the seaside at 'The Promenade Pier Café'. Experience some of the greatest events that have shaped London's heritage at 'The Spirit of London', where visitors journey through 400 years of London's history in a replica of a black taxi cab. Very busy in *Jul & Aug*. Be prepared for queues. Shop. Café. *Open 10.00-17.30 Mon-Fri (from 09.30 in summer), 09.30-17.30 Sat & Sun.* Charge (combined ticket with London Planetarium available).

Museum of London   **85 F2**

London Wall EC2. 0171-600 3699. The story of London from pre-history to present day with a variety of costumes and archaeological finds. Rooms are arranged chronologically and every item, from Roman silverwork to the Great Fire in 1666 to a 1920s Art Deco lift from Selfridges, reveals something about the history of London. Café. Shop. *Open 10.00-17.50 Tue-Sat, 12.00-17.50 Sun (last admission 17.15).* Charge.

Museum of Mankind   **82 A6**

6 Burlington Gdns W1. 0171-437 2224. Ethnographic Department of the British Museum. Contains a series of changing exhibitions on the life and culture of non-Western societies to portray the entire way of life of a particular people. Collections come from the indigenous peoples of Africa, Australia, the Pacific Islands, North and South America, and parts of Asia and Europe. A close look at the lifestyles, costumes, homes and crafts. Café. Shop. Film shows. *Open 10.00-17.00 Mon-Sat, 14.30-18.00 Sun.* Free.

Museum of the Moving Image   **95 H1**
(MOMI)

South Bank SE1. 0171-401 2636. The story of moving images from Chinese shadow puppet theatre to the beginnings of photography through to film, television, video, satellite and hologram technology. During the journey you can take part in lots of films and television-making processes. Actors and presenters help you to read the news or animate a cartoon. Frequently changing displays and plenty of moving exhibits. Restaurant. Bar.

Museum of the Moving Image (MOMI)

Café. Shop. Lectures and films. *Open 10.00-18.00 Mon-Sun (last admission 17.00).* Charge.

National Army Museum   **102 C5**

Royal Hospital Rd SW3. 0171-730 0717. The story of the British Army from 1400 to the present day. Its triumphs and disasters, professional and social life all over the world told through uniforms, pictures, weapons and even soldiers' songs at the push of a button. See a 400sq ft model of the Battle of Waterloo with over 70,000 model soldiers; also a skeleton of Napoleon's horse. Café. Shop. *Open 10.00-17.30 Mon-Sun.* Free.

National Maritime Museum

Romney Rd, Greenwich SE10. 0181-858 4422. In a beautiful riverside setting and incorporating the Old Royal Observatory and Queen's House, this is the world's finest maritime collection of paintings, navigational instruments, sea-farers' costumes and weapons. Find out all about England's great sea-faring tradition. See Nelson's uniform from the Battle of Trafalgar. *Twentieth Century Seapower* is a permanent gallery illustrating seapower on a global scale with paintings, watercolours, ship models, photographs and medals. Another major exhibition tells the story of Nelson's epic life and death. In the Old Royal Observatory stand astride the Meridian Line and reach for the sky in a dome which houses the largest refracting telescope in the UK. Café. Shop. *Open 10.00-17.00 Mon-Sun.* Charge.

Natural History Museum   **91 G6**
& Geological Museum

Cromwell Rd SW7. 0171-938 9123. The Natural History Museum houses a huge collection of animal and plant specimens; if you don't know where to start, follow one of the nature trails. The central hall houses dinosaurs, including the massive skeleton of one of the largest land animals, *Diplodocus*. Just as spectacular is the life-size model of the biggest

Natural History Museum

animal alive today – the blue whale. Learn the secrets of our planet – past and present – in 'Story of the Earth' and 'Ecology' and visit the new garden sanctuary. **The Geological Museum** houses a massive collection of gold, diamonds, minerals, rocks and fossils as well as an impressive collection of gem stones. Restaurant. Café. Shop. Both museums *open 10.00-17.50 Mon-Sat, 11.00-17.50 Sun.* Charge (free *16.30-17.50 Mon-Fri, 17.00-17.50 Sun & Bank hols*).

Pollock's Toy Museum   **72 B1**
1 Scala St W1. 0171-636 3452. The toy museum is housed in a labyrinth of tiny rooms connected by narrow winding staircases. Each room has a different theme: puppets; optical; mechanical and constructional toys; dolls and dolls' houses; teddy bears; board games; tin toys and toy theatres. Small children find the atmosphere magical, and many of the exhibits, like an Egyptian clay mouse with moving parts made about 4000 years ago, are positioned at their level. Shop. *Open 10.00-17.00 Mon-Sat (last admission 16.30).* Charge.

Science Museum   **91 G6**
Exhibition Rd SW7. 0171-938 8000. One of the three great national museums covering science, technology and medicine. Highlights of the collection include a 1797 Watts beam engine, the real Apollo 10 launch module and the oldest locomotive in the world. In the basement the children's gallery has working models demonstrating scientific principles. The Sainsbury Gallery explains the impact of science on today's food with hands-on displays, like the Food Pyramid and computer driven exhibits. The Wellcome Museum of the History of Medicine reconstructs important events in medical history and has a wealth of fascinating historical objects. The Flight Gallery records the history of aeronautics from impossible Renaissance dreams to the air transport system of today. Restaurant. Café. Shop. *Open 10.00-18.00 Mon-Sun. Closed Bank hols.* Charge (free *after 16.30*).

Shakespeare Globe Exhibition   **97 E1**
New Globe Walk, Bankside SE1. 0171-928 6406. Part of the International Globe Centre, the central focus of which will be the rebuilt Globe Theatre *(due to open in June 1996)*. In the early 17thC the original Globe Theatre on this site was the first theatre to stage several of Shakespeare's plays. Exhibition tells the story of Elizabethan theatre-going, the history of the Globe and the rebuilding project. Tour of the building site, where authentic Tudor methods are being used. *Open 10.00-17.00 Mon-Sun.* Charge.

Sherlock Holmes Museum   **80 D1**
221b Baker St NW1. 0171-935 8866. Said to be the actual house on which Conan Doyle modelled his imaginary 221b. The great detective's domestic world has been recreated, based on detailed study of the stories. See Holmes' cluttered sitting room and bedroom, full of personal touches. In Dr Watson's room you can sit by the fire and read the stories and period magazines. Shop. *Open 10.00-18.00 Mon-Sun.* Charge.

Theatre Museum   **83 F5**
Russell St WC2. 0171-836 7891. A branch of the Victoria & Albert Museum, right in the heart of 'theatreland' and the perfect place to discover the history of the English stage since the 17thC. Magnificent collection of playbills, programmes, prompt books, drawings, photographs, models, costumes and props. Café. Shop. *Open 11.00-19.00 Tue-Sun.* Charge.

Tower Bridge Museum   **98 C2**
Tower Bridge SE1. 0171-403 3761. Excellent views from the high walkways of this spectacular bridge. Exhibits bring to life the history, human endeavour and engineering achievement which created this famous landmark. The museum traces the history of the Thames bridges, including original designs for Tower Bridge, its structure and engineering. The steam pumping engines of the old hydraulics are also on display. Compare today's skyline with that of 1894 and join in

the celebrations of the Royal Opening which took place on 30 June 1894, via a light, sound and vision show. *Open Apr-Oct 10.00-18.30 Mon-Sun; Nov-Mar 10.00-17.15 Mon-Sun. Last admission 1¼ hours before closing.* Charge.

Tower Hill Pageant   **86 C3**
Tower Hill Terrace EC3. 0171-709 0081. London's first 'dark ride' museum, telling the story of 2000 years of the City of London. Automated cars take you on a journey through converted wine vaults near the Tower of London. The Pageant focuses on the riverside port area and depicts scenes from early Roman settlements to the modern docklands. See Londoners fleeing in panic before the Great Fire of 1666 and get a bird's eye view of the city from a German bomber as it blitzed the docks in 1940. *Open Apr-Oct 09.30-17.30 Mon-Sun; Nov-Mar 09.30-16.30 Mon-Sun.* Charge.

Tower of London   **86 C6**
Tower Hill EC3. 0171-709 0765. Within the famous fortress are several museums. The Tower's most valuable collection, the Crown Jewels, are housed in a display hall with moving walkways, and their story is told in audio-visual presentations. The Star of Africa is the largest cut diamond in the world. The Lower Martin Tower holds instruments of torture and the executioner's block and axe. The White Tower houses the Royal Armouries – the largest collection of medieval and Tudor

Victoria & Albert Museum

armour in Britain. Highlights include Henry VIII's armour and tilting lances; Wild West guns, including the Winchester repeater; and a huge suit of elephant armour. The Tower is also home to the museum of the Royal Regiment of Fusiliers – three small rooms packed with displays and regimental relics tell the story of the regiment from its foundation in 1685 to the present day. Shops. *Guided tours by Yeomen Warders every ½hr (except in bad weather); last tour 15.30 Mar-Oct, 14.30 Nov-Feb (included in entrance fee). Open Mar-Oct 09.00-18.00 Mon-Sat, 10.00-18.00 Sun; Nov-Feb 09.00-17.00 Mon-Sat, 10.00-17.00 Sun.* Charge.

Victoria & Albert Museum   **91 H6**
Cromwell Rd SW7. 0171-938 8500. Britain's National Museum of Art and Design has one of the world's finest collections of furniture, ceramics and glass, metalwork and jewellery, textiles and dress from the Middle Ages to the 20th century, as well as paintings, prints, drawings, posters, photographs and sculpture. The Twentieth Century Gallery spans the history of consumer design from Mackintosh fireplaces and paper dresses to Swatch watches and Dr Marten shoes. There are also superb collections from China, Japan, India and the Middle East. If you don't know what to look at first buy *100 Things to See* from the bookshop. Restaurant. Café. *Open 12.00-17.50 Mon, 10.00-17.50 Tue-Sun.* Free (donation requested).

Winston Churchill's Britain   **98 A2**
at War Experience
64-66 Tooley St SE1. 0171-403 3171. A hands-on theme museum where you can relive the drama of life in Britain during the Second World War. Journey to the London underground where many spent sleepless nights while the bombing raids went on overhead. Hear Hitler's declaration of war and Churchill's promise that Britain would never be defeated. Huddle inside an Anderson shelter and wait for the 'all-clear'. Unique display of deactivated bombs. Shop. *Open Apr-Sep 10.00-17.30 Mon-Sun; Oct-Mar 10.00-16.30 Mon-Sun.* Charge.

HISTORIC HOUSE MUSEUMS

Apsley House   **81 F3**
149 Piccadilly W1. 0171-499 5676. Originally known as 'Number One London', as it stood on the westernmost point of the city. Designed by Robert Adam, 1778, with alterations by Wyatt, 1828. Home of the 1st Duke of Wellington and now the Wellington Museum. Contains relics of Wellington's life, fine Spanish and Dutch paintings, silver plate

and porcelain. Shop. *Open 1100-17.00 Tue-Sun*. Charge.

Dickens' House   **73 G5**
48 Doughty St WC1. 0171-405 2127. Dickens lived here from 1837-9 during which time he completed *The Pickwick Papers* and wrote *Oliver Twist* and *Nicholas Nickleby*. Among the fascinating exhibits on display is the Dickens family tree, his desk, chair and china monkey, without which he couldn't start work. *Open 10.00-17.00 Mon-Sat (last admission 16.30)*. Charge.

Freud Museum
20 Maresfield Gardens, Hampstead NW3. 0171-435 2002. Exactly as it was when he died in 1939, the house Sigmund Freud found refuge in after fleeing Hitler in 1938 is perfect for analysing the analyst. Much of the furniture was brought from his home in Vienna, and the shelves are packed with his extraordinary collection of Egyptian, Greek, Roman and Oriental antiquities. In the consulting room at the back of the house is the famous couch on which psychoanalysis was pioneered. *Open 12.00-17.00 Wed-Sun*. Charge.

Dr Johnson's House   **84 B4**
17 Gough Sq, Fleet St EC4. 0171-353 3745. It was in the attic of this 17thC house that Dr Samuel Johnson compiled the first English dictionary, published in two volumes in 1755. Contains relics such as Johnson's chair from the Old Cock Tavern and a first edition of his dictionary. Shop. *Open May-Sep 11.00-17.30 Mon-Sat; Oct-Apr 11.00-17.00 Mon-Sat*. Charge.

Keats' House
Wentworth Place, Keats Grove, Hampstead NW3. 0171-435 2062. Keats lived here from 1818-20. He produced his finest poetry here, including *Ode to a Nightingale* and *La Belle Dame sans Merci*, and it was here that his love affair with Fanny Brawne began. *Open Apr-Oct 10.00-13.00 & 14.00-18.00 Mon-Fri, 10.00-13.00 & 14.00-17.00 Sat, 14.00-17.00 Sun; Nov-Mar 13.00-17.00 Mon-Fri, 10.00-13.00 & 14.00-17.00 Sat, 14.00-17.00 Sun*. Donations welcome.

Sir John Soane's Museum   **83 G3**
13 Lincoln's Inn Fields WC2. 0171-405 2107. Britain's smallest and most unusual national museum is in the former home of Sir John Soane, one of England's most respected architects. Amongst the treasures are Hogarth's paintings *The Rake's Progress* and the *Election* series; antiquities, including the sarcophagus of Seti I (1370BC) found in the Valley of the Kings; and paintings by Turner, Watteau, Reynolds and Canaletto. Shop. Guided tour *14.30 Sat*. *Open 10.00-17.00 Tue-Sat (also 18.00-21.00 1st Tue of month)*. Free.

Spencer House   **94 A2**
27 St James's Place SW1. 0171-409 0526. Built in 1756 for the first Earl Spencer, an ancestor of the Princess of Wales, the House has been restored to the splendour of its 18thC appearance. Vardy's Palm Room with its spectacular screen of gilded palm trees and arched fronds is a unique Palladian setpiece, whilst the mural decorations of the Painted Room reflect the 18thC passion for classical Greece and Rome. Murillo's *St Joseph and the Christ Child* is on view. Old master paintings from Glyndebourne are also on display. *Open Sun (except Aug & Jan) from 10.30. Guided tours only. Last tour commences 16.45*. Charge.

Wesley's House   **74 C2**
47 City Rd EC1. 0171-253 2262. John Wesley's possessions and personal relics can be found in the house, and his tomb is in the chapel he built nearby. The crypt houses a museum telling the story of Methodism. *Open 10.00-16.00 Mon-Sat, 12.00-14.00 Sun*. Guided tours. Small charge.

GALLERIES

Courtauld Institute Galleries   **83 G5**
Somerset House, Strand WC2. 0171-873 2526. Spanning 600 years of Western European art, the Institute is especially known for its Impressionist and Post-Impressionist works. Fine examples of baroque furniture, Flemish and Italian Old Masters, the Mark Gambier-Parry Bequest and works by Manet, Renoir, Cézanne, van Gogh and Gauguin. Not as crowded as some of the national galleries. Café. Shop. *Open 10.00-18.00 Mon-Sat, 14.00-18.00 Sun*. Charge.

Dulwich Picture Gallery
College Rd, Dulwich SE21. 0181-693 5254. The first public art gallery in England (1814). Includes works by Claude, Cuyp, Rembrandt (including his portrait of Jacob II de Gheyn – stolen four times), Rubens, van Dyck, Gainsborough, Hogarth, Canaletto and Watteau. Shop. Guided tour *15.00 Sat & Sun*. *Open 10.00-17.00 Tue-Fri, 11.00-17.00 Sat, 14.00-17.00 Sun. Closed Mon*. Charge.

Hayward Gallery   **95 H1**
South Bank Centre SE1. 0171-928 3144. Main venue for large-scale temporary exhibitions of both historical and contemporary American, European and British art. Café. Shop. *Open 10.00-18.00 Mon-Sun (to 20.00 Tue & Wed). Closed between exhibitions*. Charge.

National Gallery   **82 D6**
Trafalgar Sq WC2. 0171-839 3321/747 2885. Founded in 1824, the gallery houses the nation's major collection of historical paintings, covering European schools from the 13thC to 20thC. A leaflet, available at the entrance, leads you to the 16 most famous

paintings. Daily tours also highlight selected works. Famous painters include Rembrandt, Rubens, Frans Hals, van Dyck, Velázquez, El Greco, Cézanne, Monet and van Gogh. The Sainsbury Wing houses a collection of early Renaissance paintings including works by Botticelli, Raphael and Mantegna with great attention paid to the display of the paintings as well as the works themselves. Restaurant. Café/bar. Shop. *Regular guided tours Mon-Sat (contact the information desk for times). Open 10.00-18.00 Mon-Sat, 14.00-18.00 Sun. Free.*

National Portrait Gallery 82 D6
2 St Martin's Place WC2. 0171-306 0055. Portraits of famous and not so famous people throughout the ages. Start on the fifth floor and work your way down for a comprehensive, chronological look at portraits from Richard II to Mick Jagger via Nell Gwynne, William Shakespeare, Winston Churchill and the present Royal Family. The collection includes sculptures, miniatures, drawings and caricatures. Bookshop. *Open 10.00-18.00 Mon-Sat, 12.00-18.00 Sun. Closed some Bank hols. Free.*

Queen's Gallery 93 H4
Buckingham Palace, Buckingham Palace Rd SW1. 0171-839 1377. This annexe to Buckingham Palace contains exhibits selected from the Royal art collection, regarded as one of the world's finest. Selections, changed at intervals, may include works by Rembrandt, Vermeer, Rubens, Holbein and Canaletto, as well as Sèvres porcelain, stamps and drawings. Shop. *Open 09.30-16.30 Mon-Sun. Closed Bank hols.* Charge.

Royal Academy of Arts 82 A6
Burlington House, Piccadilly W1. 0171-439 7438. Holds a series of important special-loan exhibitions throughout the year. Famous for its annual 'Summer Exhibition' which displays thousands of works by living artists for view and sale. Can get very crowded at weekends. Restaurant. Shop. *Open 10.00-18.00 Mon-Sun (last admission 17.30).* Charge.

Tate Gallery 105 E2
Millbank SW1. 0171-887 8000. Sir Henry Tate donated his own collection of paintings together with $80,000 for a new building in 1891. Exhibits British paintings from 16thC to present day, plus world art from 1880 onwards. The adjoining Clore Gallery houses the Turner Collection, 300 paintings and 20,000 drawings by J.M.W. Turner. Due to the size of its collection, the Tate operates a policy of annual rotation, as they can only show a percentage of the works at any one time. Restaurant. Café. Shop. *Guided tours Mon-Fri (contact the information desk for times). Open 10.00-17.50 Mon-Sat, 14.00-17.50 Sun. Free (charge for special exhibitions).*

Wallace Collection 81 E3
Hertford House, Manchester Sq W1. 0171-935 0687. A private collection of outstanding works of art which was bequeathed to the nation by Lady Wallace in 1897. Splendid representation of the French 17thC and 18thC artists, including paintings by Fragonard, Watteau and Boucher. Home to the *Laughing Cavalier* by Frans Hals and also works by Rembrandt, Titian, Rubens, Canaletto and Guardi. Important collections of French furniture, Sèvres porcelain, majolica, Limoges enamel and armour. Shop. *Tours by prior arrangement. Open 10.00-17.00 Mon-Sat, 14.00-17.00 Sun. Closed some Bank hols. Free.*

Tate Gallery

*R*oyal London

London is rich in royal connections. Since 1066 every British monarch has been crowned at Westminster Abbey and has maintained a royal residence in the capital or just outside, such as at Windsor. After hundreds of years of influence, the Royal Family have left their mark on the capital through palaces, memorials, foundations and even streets. Anyone prepared to stand on the right pavement at the appropriate time may see the Queen herself, and possibly members of her family, pass by in a car or carriage.

ROYAL PAGEANTS

DAILY CEREMONIES

Ceremony of the Keys   **86 C6**
Tower of London EC3. 0171-709 0765. Although not attended by a royal, this nightly 7-minute long ceremony of locking the Tower was originally begun to guard the monarch against 'the unruly London mob'. The West Gate, the Middle Tower and the Byward Tower are ceremoniously locked by the Chief Warder of the Yeomen Warders at *21.40* and the Last Post is sounded at *22.00*. *Attendance is by written application only, well in advance and enclosing a stamped addressed envelope* *(sae) to the Resident Governor, Queen's House, HM Tower of London EC3.* Free.

Changing the Guard   **94 A4**
Buckingham Palace SW1. This colourful and entertaining ceremony takes place inside the palace railings at *11.30 every day in summer, alternate days in winter*. See the old guard of the Foot Guards (who were once responsible for protecting the monarch's life) change duty at Buckingham Palace. Also at **Whitehall** (**95 E2**) at *11.00 Mon-Sat, 10.00 Sun*, and **Windsor Castle**, Windsor, Berks (01753) 868286 at *11.00 Mon-Sat in summer, alternate days in winter*. Free.

STATE OCCASIONS

Although not state occasions, there are several annual events which members of the Royal Family attend. **Royal Ascot** in *mid Jun* is attended by the Queen and most members of the Royal Family. **Henley Royal Regatta** in *Jul* is attended by several members. At the **Wimbledon Lawn Tennis Championships** in *Jun/Jul* the Duke and Duchess of Kent award the trophies. In *Mar* at the **Royal Film Performance**, a member of the Royal Family attends a special screening of a film selected for Royal patronage. Usually at one of the cinemas in Leicester Square (**83 D6**).

Changing the Guard

State Opening of Parliament   95 F5

House of Lords, Houses of Parliament SW1. In *early Nov*, Her Majesty The Queen is driven in the Irish State Coach, from Buckingham Palace (leaving about *10.30*) along the Mall, Horse Guards' Parade, through Admiralty Arch and down Whitehall to the House of Lords. Marking the new parliamentary year, the procession ends at the throne in the Lord's Chamber from where the Queen's Speech, outlining the Government's programme for the coming session, is read. Good views of the outside procession from the north side of The Mall.

Trooping the Colour   95 E2

Horse Guards' Parade, Whitehall SW1. Pageantry at its best for the Queen's Official Birthday in *Jun*. On this day the Queen assumes both the role of Sovereign and Colonel-in-Chief of the seven regiments of the Household Division and inspects the colour (flag) of one of them. The procession leaves Buckingham Palace (at about *10.30*) and goes along The Mall to Horse Guards' Parade and Whitehall and back again. After the *11.00* ceremony the Royal Family watch an RAF 'fly past' from the balcony of Buckingham Palace. Be prepared for crowds outside the railings. *Tickets available from the Brigade Major, Trooping the Colour, Household Division, Horse Guards' Parade SW1. Apply well in advance and enclose a stamped addressed envelope (sae). Sat nearest 11 Jun.* Charge.

ROYAL RESIDENCES

Several of the royal palaces in or near London are open to the public. The most famous royal residence is Buckingham Palace. The State Apartments at the Palace are open to the public in *Aug & Sep*. The Queen usually moves to her residences (other than Buckingham Palace – which is the principal one) at fairly regular times. Sandringham for *New Year* and *Jan*; Windsor Castle from *mid Mar-May & Jun*; Holyroodhouse, Edinburgh from *end Jun-beg Jul*; Balmoral for *Aug & Sep*; Windsor Castle for family Christmas from *mid-end Dec*. Foreign visits tend to take place *Oct-Nov & Feb-Mar*. The Royal Standard flies when the Queen is in residence.

Buckingham Palace   45 H4

St James's Park SW1. Built in 1705, it was originally Buckingham House. George IV commissioned an enlargement, headed by the archi-

Her Majesty Queen Elizabeth II

tect, John Nash. This started around 1819 but was not completed until 1837, by which time Queen Victoria was on the throne. Even then it was not fit to live in, with faulty drains, doors which wouldn't open and thousands of windows which wouldn't shut! It has been a royal residence ever since – Edward VII was born and died here and George VI was bombed in it during the Blitz. It has 600 rooms although only 12 are occupied by Queen Elizabeth II and the Duke of Edinburgh. The Royal Standard flies when the Queen is in residence. The Changing of the Guard takes place in the forecourt – see page 24. There are private garden parties held each *summer* in the extensive gardens. Apartments *open Aug & Sep 09.30-17.30 Mon-Sun. Phone 0171-930 5526 for tickets.* For Queen's Gallery details, see page 23.

Clarence House   46 B3

Stable Yard Gate SW1. William IV first occupied this elegant, stuccoed house by Nash (1825) as he considered Buckingham Palace too grand. Since then it has been home to many royals – Queen Victoria's mother; her second son, Prince Alfred the Duke of Edinburgh; and Queen Elizabeth II, who lived here from 1947-50 before her accession to the throne. Princess Anne was born here and it is now the home of Her Majesty Queen

Buckingham Palace

Elizabeth the Queen Mother. On her birthday, 4 August, she greets well-wishers at the gate. *Not open to the public.*

Hampton Court Palace

East Molesey, Surrey. 0181-781 9500. Built in 1514 for Cardinal Thomas Wolsey, who presented it to Henry VIII to try to regain favour after he refused to annul the king's marriage to Catherine of Aragon. For his pains he had his entire goods and lands appropriated by the king in 1529 and died on the way to imprisonment in the Tower of London. The palace has a long history of royal inhabitants from Henry VIII in 1529 to George II in 1760.

Hampton Court Palace

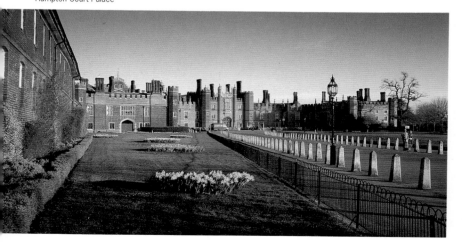

Kensington Palace

Edward VI was born here, Elizabeth I began the gardens with rare plants such as tobacco and the potato brought to her from abroad by Ralegh and Drake. Parts of the palace were rebuilt by Wren under William III and Mary and the interior was decorated by a team of the best artists and craftsmen of the day – Tijou, Verrio, Grinling Gibbons and Laguerre. Queen Victoria declared it open to the public in 1838. It also houses a rare 'real tennis' court (still used) on which Henry VIII once played. In the grounds are the Orangery, the Great Vine and the famous Maze in which it is all too easy to get lost! The formal gardens are probably among the greatest in the world. Be prepared for queues. *Open mid Apr-Sep 09.30-18.00 Mon-Sun; Oct-Mar 10.15-18.00 Mon, 09.30-16.30 Tue-Sun.* Charge.

Kensington Palace   **42 D2**
Kensington Gardens W8. 0171-937 9561. Bought by William III in 1689 and added to by Wren. The Orangery House was built by Hawksmoor and Vanbrugh for Queen Anne in 1704. Restoration took place under George I, but it then fell into disrepair during George III's reign as he preferred Buckingham Palace. Queen Victoria was born here in 1819 and in 1837 it was here that she was told she had become Queen of England. On her 70th birth-

day the State Apartments were opened to the public. Many apartments are still used by members of the Royal Family. State Apartments and Costume Museum *open 09.00-17.00 Mon-Sat, 11.00-17.00 Sun (last admission 16.15).* Charge. *Closed for refurbishment until May 1996.*

St James's Palace   **46 B2**
Pall Mall SW1. Built by Henry VIII for Anne Boleyn, his second wife and mother of Elizabeth I. Their initials can be seen above the gatehouse door. Used as a royal palace for over 300 years, it became the principal royal residence after the Palace of Whitehall was destroyed by fire in 1698. It has officially remained a royal residence although no members of the Royal Family live there at present. It provides residences for various officers of the royal household and is divided into four courts with the remains of the original palace in Colour Court. Queen Mary died here, Charles I spent the last night before his execution here, and Queen Victoria and Georges III, IV and V were all married here! Foreign ambassadors and High Commissioners are still accredited to the Court of St James's although they are now received at Buckingham Palace. State rooms *not open to the public.* Courtyards *open to the public.* Free.

Windsor Castle

Windsor, Berks. (01753) 868286. An imposing 800-year-old medieval fortress, adjoining nearly 5000 acres of Windsor Great Park and gardens. Most parts of the castle are open to the public. Of all the royal palaces, this has been the most consistently occupied. The Queen is in official residence here for at least a quarter of the year, at *Christmas*, for parts of *March, April and May* and in *June* for Royal Ascot Week and the Garter Service in St George's Chapel. Not to be missed is Queen Mary's Dolls' House – the palace in perfect miniature – designed by Sir Edwin Lutyens. 12thC Round Tower built by Henry II. St George's Chapel is fine 16thC perpendicular. Opening times depend on the movements of the Royal Family and ceremonial occasions, so it is advisable to check with the Castle Information Office. State Apartments and castle precinct *open Apr-Oct 10.00-15.00 Mon-Sun; Nov-Mar 10.00-14.00 Mon-Sun.* Charge.

St James's Palace

Windsor Castle

London's River

The Thames has been London's lifeline for 2000 years and was instrumental in the Roman settlement, which created London as an international port. Once used as the local bypass, being cheaper and safer than travel by road, it has carried Viking longships, Roman galleys, Elizabethan barges and Victorian steamers. It bore witness to the treasures brought back by travellers and saw the departure of ships setting off to trade and fight.

One of the best ways to see London is still from the Thames. Although no longer used as an international port (cargo ships now use Tilbury as they are too big to come further upstream) the Thames has once again become a busy highway, full of pleasure cruisers and commuter boats. The buildings and sights lining its twisting, turning path are as varied as London itself; through them the history of the capital unfolds.

RIVERBUS

Thames Commuter Services
Tavern House, Cannon Drive, Hertsmere Rd E14. 0171-537 4374. The riverbus travels between Festival Pier and Canary Wharf, via London Bridge City Pier, at peak commuting times *Mon-Fri only:*
Services from Festival Pier to Canary Wharf *07.30-09.30 every 15 mins;* return journey from Canary Wharf to Festival Pier *16.45-19.00 every 15 mins.*

Festival Pier	**95 G1**
London Bridge City Pier	**98 A1**

RIVER TRIPS

Daily services run from the piers listed below, but you may board at any of the other piers en route. It is important to note that times vary according to the tides and the weather and it's always advisable to phone for details first. *Always check the times of return boats at the pier on arrival.*

DOWNRIVER SERVICES

Charing Cross Pier   **95 F1**
Victoria Embankment WC2. 0171-839 3572. Trips to the Tower (*20-minute journey*) and Greenwich (*45-minute journey*) *every 30 minutes Apr-Oct 10.30-16.00 Mon-Sun; every 45 minutes Nov-Mar 10.30-15.00 Mon-Sun.* 2-hour luncheon cruise *12.45 Sun only, all year.*

Greenwich Pier
Return services to Charing Cross Pier (*45-minute journey*), Tower Pier (*30-minute journey*) and Westminster Pier (*45-minute journey*). Telephone the individual piers for details.

Tower Pier   **98 B1**
0171-488 0344. Trips to Greenwich (*30-minute journey*) *every 20 minutes 11.00-17.00 in summer (every 40 minutes Nov-Mar) Mon-Sun;* to Westminster (*25-minute journey*) *every 20 minutes 11.00-18.00 in summer (every 40 minutes 11.00-17.00 Nov-Mar) Mon-Sun.* Ferry to HMS *Belfast* (*5-minute journey*) *every 15 minutes in summer only.* Ferry service enquiries 0171-407 6434.

Westminster Pier   **95 F3**
Victoria Embankment SW1. 0171-930 4097. Trips to the Tower (*30-minute journey*) *every 20 minutes 10.30-16.00 Mon-Sun* and to Greenwich (*40-minute journey*) *every 30 minutes 10.30-16.00; all year.* Special trips to the Thames Flood Barrier (*75-minute journey each way*) *10.00, 11.15, 12.40, 13.45 & 15.15 Apr-Oct.* Disco cruises *19.00 Fri & 20.00 Sat; all year.*

UPRIVER SERVICES

Westminster Pier   **95 F3**
Victoria Embankment SW1. 0171-930 4721. Westminster Passenger Services operate boat trips to Putney (*30-minute journey*), Kew (*90-minute journey*), Richmond (*2-hr journey*) and Hampton Court (*3-4 hr journey*) *during summer only.* Phone 0171-930 2062 for departure times.
There are local services to Hampton Court (*Easter-Sep*) from Richmond and Kingston. Phone 0181-546 2434 for details.

THE RIVER THAMES

Evening on the Thames

N. Daly

NORTH BANK

Magnificent 2 **Hampton Court Palace**, built by Cardinal Wolsey and the favourite country residence of Henry VIII, is bordered by 3 **Hampton Court Park**. Embarking at Barge Walk, by 1 **Hampton Court Bridge**, you can get a good idea of what travelling to London was like for the royal residents. 4 **Bushy Park** was enclosed by Cardinal Wolsey as part of the Hampton Court estate. Opened to the public by Queen Victoria in 1838, it is indeed wild and bushy! Hampton Wick, to the left, is a residential area, part of the general parish of Hampton. Around the bend lies the beginning of the end of leafy suburbia with 8 **Teddington Lock**. From here towards London the Thames is tidal. Teddington, another residential area, has the Thames TV Studios, housed in a riverside mansion next to the Weir.

The Thames at Hampton

SOUTH BANK

Behind the pretty white arches of 5 **Kingston Bridge** lies Kingston, an early fishing village, market town and royal borough with a wide range of shops and a good river frontage. Passing 6 **Stevens Eyot** and 7 **Trowlock Island**, all around is rural greenery. 8 **Teddington Lock** marks the beginning of the tidal Thames. To the east is Ham, a largely residential area with parkland bordering the river. Within the parkland is 10 palatial, flamboyant **Ham House**, built in 1610 by Sir Thomas Vavasour for the Earls of Dysart. Owned by the National Trust, it has been restored to its full baroque splendour.

HAM

Teddington
Footbridge

HAMPTON
WICK

Kingston
Bridge

BUSHY
PARK

Hampton
Court
Bridge

HAMPTON
COURT
PARK

KINGST

Twickenham, past Strawberry Hill, the Gothic home of Horace Walpole, offers beautiful riverside settings. The path of the river is dotted with several willow-covered islands, among them **9 Eel Pie Island**. The Twickenham **ferry 11** still runs from the Boat House to Ham House. **12 Marble Hill House**, an 18thC Palladian villa, looms gracefully from its spacious riverside park. Built by George II's mistress, Henrietta Howard, the gardens were designed by Alexander Pope and Charles Bridgman. Through Richmond (see south bank) is **16 Richmond Lock** and **Footbridge**, with good riverside walks. Isleworth, by **17 Isleworth Ait**, became a fashionable place to live in the 18thC with several grand riverside estates. Vincent van Gogh taught here and used the Thames as the subject for his first attempts at painting. **18** The **London Apprentice** pub, built around 1741, is part of a charming setting with

the 15thC tower of All Saint's Church and several Georgian houses. As the river bends, a delightful landscape unfolds, with **20 Syon House** set in Syon Park behind wooded banks to the north and the Royal Botanic Gardens to the south. Syon House, the seat of the Percy family since 1594, has magnificent interiors and grounds designed by Capability Brown sweeping down to the river. Heading towards **25 Kew Bridge** is Brentford, an important area due to its situation on the main route west from London. **22** The **Grand Union Canal**, a direct

link to Birmingham, still joins the Thames here, although it is no longer busy with commercial traffic. Past Kew Bridge, the residential area of Chiswick is fronted by **26 Strand-on-the-Green**, a riverside path with several notable and attractive 18thC houses, once home to many famous residents including Nancy Mitford, William Morris and Dylan Thomas. Flooding was common here at high tide until the construction of the Thames Barrier. There are also two riverside pubs, the City Barge, a 15thC charter inn, and the 350-year-old Bull's Head.

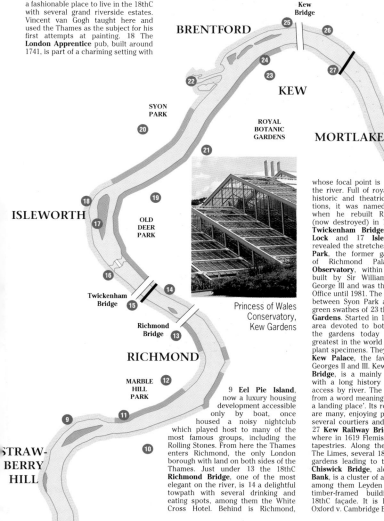

Princess of Wales Conservatory, Kew Gardens

whose focal point is the river. Full of royal, historic and theatrical associations, it was named by Henry VII when he rebuilt Richmond Palace (now destroyed) in 1497. Passing **15 Twickenham Bridge**, **16 Richmond Lock** and **17 Isleworth Ait** are revealed the stretches of **21 Old Deer Park**, the former garden and park of Richmond Palace. **19 Kew Observatory**, within the park, was built by Sir William Chambers for George III and was the Meteorological Office until 1981. The river now passes between Syon Park and the glorious green swathes of **23** the **Royal Botanic Gardens**. Started in 1759 with a small area devoted to botanic collections, the gardens today are among the greatest in the world with over 25,000 plant specimens. They also contain **24 Kew Palace**, the favourite home of Georges II and III. Kew, behing **25 Kew Bridge**, is a mainly residential area with a long history due to its easy access by river. The name is derived from a word meaning 'neck of land by a landing place'. Its royal associations are many, enjoying popularity with several courtiers and monarchs. Past **27 Kew Railway Bridge** is Mortlake, where in 1619 Flemish weavers made tapestries. Along the waterfront are The Limes, several attractive 18thC houses with gardens leading to the river. By **28 Chiswick Bridge**, along **29 Thames Bank**, is a cluster of attractive houses, among them Leyden House, a 15thC timber-framed building behind an 18thC façade. It is here the annual Oxford v. Cambridge Boat Race ends.

9 Eel Pie Island, now a luxury housing development accessible only by boat, once housed a noisy nightclub which played host to many of the most famous groups, including the Rolling Stones. From here the Thames enters Richmond, the only London borough with land on both sides of the Thames. Just under **13** the 18thC **Richmond Bridge**, one of the most elegant on the river, is **14** a delightful towpath with several drinking and eating spots, among them the White Cross Hotel. Behind is Richmond,

Kew Bridge

BRENTFORD

25

26

24

23

27

22

KEW

SYON PARK

ROYAL BOTANIC GARDENS

MORTLAKE

20

21

Chiswick Bridge

28

29

18

19

ISLEWORTH

17

OLD DEER PARK

16

Twickenham Bridge

15

14

Richmond Bridge

13

RICHMOND

MARBLE HILL PARK

12

9

11

10

STRAW-BERRY HILL

Boats moored at the riverside gardens of grand 18thC houses on **31 Chiswick Mall** are a continuing reminder of the wealthy riverside village it once was. Similar houses line the banks along **32 Upper Mall** and **33 Lower Mall**, where there are several popular historic pubs – the Blue Anchor, the Dove (whose past imbibers include Nell Gwynne, Graham Greene and Ernest Hemingway), the 17thC Old Ship – and several rowing clubs. **37 Riverside Bishops Park** is home to Fulham Palace, the official residence of the Bishop of London until 1973. Plane trees border the pleasant riverside walk within the park. Exclusive and expensive riverside apartments by Putney Bridge are followed by Hurlingham Park with **39 Hurlingham House**, dating to 1760. With a fine river frontage, it became a private sports club where the wealthy enjoyed polo, croquet and tennis – and still do! Under **41 Wandsworth Bridge** and past Battersea Reach is **42 Chelsea Harbour**, offering smart shops, apartments, restaurants and a marina. **44 Chelsea Wharf** has been transformed from old warehouses into modern business units. Fashionable **45 Cheyne Walk** is still a smart address, where grand houses were occupied by such famous former residents as Isambard Kingdom Brunel, Hilaire Belloc and James Whistler. Chelsea Old Church, the last resting place of Sir Thomas More, lies on its western point. Beyond Albert Bridge is **46 Chelsea Royal Hospital**, established by Charles II for veteran soldiers. It opened in 1689, admitting 476 army pensioners. The Chelsea Flower Show is held in the grounds annually in May. Behind the wharfs of Pimlico and **50 Pimlico Gardens** lies genteel residential charm. Past **52 Vauxhall Bridge**, the first iron bridge to span the Thames, is **54** the Tate Gallery, housing the national collection of modern and British art. It stands on the site of the Millbank Penitentiary, where criminals awaited boats to carry them downriver to be deported to Australia. Next door is **55 Vickers Tower**, one of London's earliest glass-walled office skyscrapers (1960-63). **58** Augustus Pugin and Charles Barry's magnificent **Houses of Parliament** have a prime site right by Westminster Bridge. In 1856 the 'Great Stink' from untreated sewage in the river became so bad that canvases soaked in chloride of lime were hung at the windows to counteract the smell. Nowadays, in summer, you can see MPs on the terraces taking refreshment and entertaining their guests. The best way to view the building is moving upstream from Westminster Pier. **60 Victoria Embankment** was created by Sir Joseph Bazalgette in 1868 by reclaiming 37 acres (15.4ha) of mud. This made the river narrower and the water flow faster, so ending the skating era on the once-frozen waters. Halfway along the Embankment are **61 Whitehall Stairs**, once part of Whitehall Palace (destroyed by fire in 1698). Cardinal Wolsey descended these steps to be rowed to Henry VIII at Greenwich, and in 1688 James II escaped by them from William of Orange. There are several ships along this stretch: **62 PS Tattershall Castle**, once a paddle-steamer, now converted into a restaurant and bar, **65 RS Hispaniola**, once a ferry on the Firth of Clyde in Scotland and now a restaurant, and **66 TS Queen Mary**, a pub and functions venue. Embankment Place, above Charing Cross Station, and the vaults below the station, house retail outlets and restaurants. The imposing gateway on the

Chelsea Wharf

Hammersmith Bridge
The original was the first suspension bridge in London. Built in 1824 by William T. Clarke, it was replaced in 1883 by the present construction, by Sir Joseph Bazalgette. In 1939 the IRA tried to blow it up, but the plot was foiled by a passer-by who threw the bomb into the river.

Albert Bridge

N. Daly

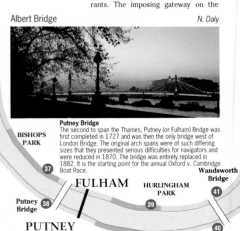

Putney Bridge
The second to span the Thames, Putney (or Fulham) Bridge was first completed in 1727 and was then the only bridge west of London Bridge. The original arch spans were of such differing sizes that they presented serious difficulties for navigators and were reduced in 1870. The bridge was entirely replaced in 1882. It is the starting point for the annual Oxford v. Cambridge Boat Race.

On the edge of the loop is **30 Barnes Terrace**, behind whose attractive ironwork façades lies delightful Barnes village. The terrace was, and still is a fashionable place to live, with former residents including Sheridan and Gustav Holst. At the tip of Barnes is **34 St Paul's School**, an exclusive public school founded originally in 1509 by the Dean of St Paul's Cathedral. Famous pupils include John Milton, Samuel Pepys, Judge Jeffreys and Edmond Halley, the astronomer. Past Hammersmith Bridge is **35 Harrods Repository**, formerly a storage depot of the great shop. **36 Barn Elms Reservoir** is host to a variety of watersports, particularly sailing and windsurfing, and is part of Barn Elms Park, from where there are good riverside walks leading into Putney. Along Putney Embankment are several rowing clubs – the Oxford v. Cambridge Boat Race starts from here. By **38 Putney Pier** are some good pubs,

BARNES

FULHAM

PUTNEY

WANDSWORTH

Hammersmith Bridge

BISHOPS PARK

HURLINGHAM PARK

Putney Bridge

Wandsworth Bridge

31
32 33
34
35
36
30
37
38
39
40
41

north side of Victoria Embankment Gardens is **66 York Watergate**, built in 1626 by Nicholas Stone as the riverside entrance to York House which once had gardens sweeping down to the Thames. It marks the position of the north bank of the Thames before the construction of the Victoria Embankment. The rooftops of **68** the Savoy Hotel are clearly discernible from the river just before Waterloo Bridge. The famous and the wealthy still stay here in order to enjoy some of the best views of the Thames. It was from one of the hotel's balconies that Claude Monet painted 18 canvases of Waterloo Bridge. Just by the Savoy is **67 Cleopatra's Needle**, a 60ft (18m)-high ancient Egyptian granite

Cleopatra's Needle

obelisk brought to London by sea in 1878. When it was erected various articles were buried beneath it for posterity – the morning's newspapers, a razor, coins, four Bibles in different languages and photographs of '12 of the best-looking Englishwomen of the day'. The bronze sphinxes were added (facing the wrong way!) in 1882. **70 Thames Sailing Barge Wilfred** at Temple Stairs, is now a restaurant. **71 Somerset House** stands on the site of an unfinished Renaissance palace. Best seen from the river, its long, elegant façade is a magnificent landmark. The river once lapped against its terraces and through river entrances, but is now separated from it by Embankment. After

a long history of royal inhabitants, it houses offices of the Inland Revenue, and the Courtauld Institute Galleries. Just before Blackfriars Bridge is **72 HMS President**, once used by the Royal Naval Reserve and now housing an educational charity.

Blackfriars Bridge
Built in 1760, and the third bridge to span the Thames. It cost £230,000 and was mainly paid for by fines which had accumulated from men refusing the post of Sheriff! In 1860 it was replaced by the present structure, opened by Queen Victoria. She was apparently so unpopular at the time that on her way to the grand opening the crowds hissed at her in the Strand.

Westminster Bridge
The watermen of the Thames were paid £25,000 in compensation when construction of this stone bridge began in 1738. When it opened in 1750 a stern warning went out – no dogs and the death penalty for anyone found defacing its walls! The present structure is cast iron and was built in 1854-62 to a design by Thomas Page.

Lambeth Bridge
The site of the first bridge at Lambeth was originally the only place where it was possible to cross the river with a coach and horses. Unfortunately, in 1633 Archbishop Laud sank the ferry with his belongings whilst moving into Lambeth Palace. The first bridge here was constructed in 1861 and replaced in 1929.

Battersea Bridge
The original bridge (1771) was wooden and replaced the regular ferry between Chelsea and Battersea, thus transforming Chelsea from a village to a thriving small town. The original bridge was replaced in 1886-90 by the present one, designed by Sir Joseph Bazalgette.

Chelsea Bridge
The original bridge was built in 1858 by Thomas Page. Human bones and Roman and British weapons found during excavations around the bridge tell of an immense battle. It was entirely replaced in 1934 by another suspension bridge (Rendel, Palmer and Tritton).

Albert Bridge
A three-span bridge constructed in 1871 by R.M. Ordish. It was strengthened in 1971 to increase traffic loads. Tradition has it that soldiers crossing must break step because their marching rhythm may weaken the structure! It is particularly beautiful at night when illuminated.

among them the Duke's Head and the Star and Garter. Putney Bridge originally linked old Fulham to the once farming and fishing community at Putney. Early commuters included Tudor merchants from their riverside houses; now they are of a different kind, packing into crowded tubes to head for the city. The once rural village of Wandsworth, named after the tributary, the River Wandle, now presents an industrial, somewhat drab scene. Past residents include Defoe, Thackeray and Voltaire. There's a good pub, **40** the **Ship**, just by Wandsworth Bridge. Several wharfs and

jetties along this part of the river are testament to the days of thriving trade – Huguenot refugees settled here making hats and dying cloth in the 18thC. Battersea Bridge joined Battersea, famous for its market gardens, to fashionable Chelsea. There are pleasant riverside walks here and, in the vestry of **43** the riverside **Church of St Mary**, J.M.W. Turner sat and watched the sunsets across the river. Past pretty Albert Bridge lies **48 Battersea Park**, with **47** the striking **London Peace Pagoda** by the river. The only pagoda in London, it is also the only monument in Britain dedicated to world peace. Past Chelsea Bridge is **49 Battersea Power Station**, now disused and looking, some say, like an upturned snooker table! Although somewhat ugly, it is a remarkable landmark and plans are afoot to redevelop it for office and leisure use. Industrial areas now loom on the banks with busy Nine Elms Lane, on which stands **51 New Covent Garden Market**, moved in 1974 from its central London site. Beyond Vauxhall Bridge is **Vauxhall**

Cross, 10 layered storeys of Government offices, built of glass. Beyond Lambeth Bridge you can see **55** the Tudor gatehouse of impressive Gothic **Lambeth Palace**, the official residence of the Archbishop of Canterbury since 1197. **56 St Thomas's Hospital**, named after Thomas à Becket, originally had strict rules: patients were only fed if they went daily to chapel and no person could be admitted for the same disease twice! Florence Nightingale established her nursing school here. On the other side of Westminster Bridge is **58 County Hall**, a massive edifice designed in 1911 for the Greater London Council (abolished in 1986). Partly converted into luxury flats, there are plans to turn the rest – including 2100ft (640m) river frontage – into a hotel and leisure complex. **62 Hungerford Railway Bridge** has excellent views from its footbridge and next to it is **63** the **South Bank Centre** with the Royal Festival Hall, RFH2 (Queen Elizabeth Hall, RFH3 (Purcell Room), National Film Theatre and, nestling behind, the Hayward Gallery. Past Waterloo Bridge is **69** the **National Theatre** with the **Museum of the Moving Image** beside it. As concrete is the dominating material, many regard the buildings as somewhat unattractive in appearance. **74 Gabriel's Wharf** is a lively market, the south bank's answer to Covent Garden. **75** The art deco **'OXO' Tower** contains an unusual mixture of community housing, shops, workshops, cafes and offices.

Waterloo Bridge
Originally built in 1811 by Rennie and opened on the anniversary of the Battle of Waterloo. It was named Strand Bridge but changed in 1816 to its present name to emulate a great and glorious achievement – the Battle of Waterloo. The present bridge was designed by Sir Giles Gilbert Scott and constructed in 1937-42.

VICTORIA EMBANKMENT GARDENS

Waterloo Bridge

Blackfriars Bridge

71 72

66 67 68 70

65 64 69

61 63 74 75

59 62 60 58

Westminster Bridge 57

56 55

Lambeth Bridge

54

53

Vauxhall Bridge

52

PIMLICO GARDENS

Chelsea Bridge

50 51

46

47

48

BATTERSEA PARK

Albert Bridge

45

43

Battersea Bridge

As you round the corner, you can see the dome and spire of St Paul's Cathedral and the NatWest Tower rising above the rooftops of the City. With the towering monoliths of the City behind is London Bridge and **80 Fishmongers' Hall**, dedicated to the Worshipful Company of Fishmongers, one of the 96 City Livery companies. On the other side of London Bridge is **81 Monument**, a Doric column 202ft (61.5m) high commemorating the Great Fire of London. Along this stretch, and set back from the river, is **82 Waterman's Hall**, founded for the watermen of the City of London, who once operated all water transport. They had the monopoly on passenger carriage until the arrival of hackney coaches, sedan chairs and more bridges, which obviated the need for ferries. The company is still active. **85 The Tower of London** lies solid and forbidding by Tower Bridge. It is easy to imagine the terror of the criminals as they were brought silently downriver through Traitors' Gate to await their fate. Elizabeth I would have had a particularly distressing arrival seeing the head of her mother, Anne Boleyn, on a spike at the gate. Today it is a lot safer to disembark and explore

London's oldest medieval fortress. Tower Bridge marks the beginning of London's Docklands. Stretching from Tower Pier to Beckton (off map), the area has undergone massive change from a thriving, commercial port through closure to regeneration. The London Docklands Development Corporation (LDDC) was set up in 1981 to create a 'new city for the 21stC' with riverside apartments, shops, restaurants and offices. Despite great controversy many of the plans have come to fruition – warehouses that once stored spices and tobacco now house jacuzzis, saunas, satellite televisions and high-tech equipment. **86 St Katharine's Dock** was the first of the docks to be rejuvenated. Built on 23 acres (9.5ha), the original docks were closed down in 1968. Five years later an $80 million building scheme was begun which included **87 the Tower Thistle Hotel** (a somewhat bleak construction) and the World Trade Centre. The magnificent warehouses have been restored and now house shops, apartments, offices, restaurants, a yacht club and marina. Visiting cruisers nestling alongside resident yachts, and barges invoke an almost holiday atmosphere. The Dickens Inn is a particularly popular drinking spot. Wapping is a mainly residential area with a good selection of

The City skyline with the NatWest Tower

Tower Bridge   *N. Daly*
Completed in 1894, Sir Horace Jones and John Wolfe-Barry designed this dramatic Victorian-Gothic bridge to echo the Tower of London. It opens to allow tall ships to pass. Each section of the double-bascule drawbridge weighs over 1000 tonnes but can be raised in under two minutes. The high walkways afford excellent views of London and the Thames.

Southwark Bridge
London Bridge

76 78 77
80 81 82
85 86
79 83 87
84

WAPPING
93
91 92
96

Southwark Bridge
Built in response to the need for a bridge between London and Blackfriars bridges in 1814. It is the largest bridge ever constructed of cast iron, indeed the ironworkers were bankrupted by the job! It was replaced in 1912-21 by the present steel construction.

Tower Bridge
88
89
90
94 95

London Bridge
London Bridge reigned supreme for 500 years, originally a wooden construction built by the Romans. This was replaced with a stone one in the 12thC, which carried houses, shops and the heads of traitors on spikes. Among them were Thomas More, Thomas Cromwell and the rebel Jack Cade. The bridge has been replaced many times and in 1971 the granite construction by Rennie (1832) was shipped off in its entirety to Lake Havasu City, Arizona. The present bridge dates from 1973.

Rotherhithe Tunnel
Built 1904-8 by Sir Maurice Fitzmaurice and still used as a thoroughfare. The top of the tunnel is 48ft (14.5m) below the high-water mark to allow for large ships passing above.

ROTHERHITHE

BERMONDSEY

From **77 Bankside** are fine views of St Paul's Cathedral and the City. Wren lodged at no.49 while his cathedral and city were being built after the Great Fire of 1666. Dominated by **78 Bankside Power Station** – soon to become the Tate Gallery of Modern Art – there are riverside walks here and **76 the Anchor**, an historic pub with strong smuggling connections, built in 1770. Nearby is the reconstructed Shakespeare's Globe, now holding regular performances. Just before London Bridge is **79 the** schooner **Kathleen & May**, moored in St Mary Overy Dock. It is the last surviving three-masted, topsail, trading schooner. In the Pool of London is the vast **83 HMS Belfast**, the largest and most powerful warship ever built for the Royal Navy. Behind it is **84 the London Bridge City** development, incorporating Hay's Galleria, a large

converted warehouse. Disembark here for shopping, eating and drinking. A major new theatre is being built beside Tower Bridge. **88 Butler's Wharf**, is dominated by the Gastrodome, Terence Conran's complex of three restaurants and adjoining food shops. **89** The **Design Museum**, charting designs past and present, is further along. There are few docks on the south bank, although the transformation of **90 St Saviour's Dock** won an award. Bermondsey (inland, behind St Saviour's Dock) has retained a good deal of its old dockland atmosphere, as has Rotherhithe which is named from two Saxon words 'redhra' – mariner, and ''hyth'' – haven, and started life as a small maritime settlement along the river. By **94 Cherry Garden Pier**, where a ship sounds her horn if she needs Tower Bridge opened, and from where J.M.W.

Turner painted *The Fighting Temeraire*, is **95** the historic **Angel** pub. It dates from the 15thC with part of the inn built on piles over the river. Trapdoors in the floor were once used by smugglers and 'Hanging' Judge Jeffreys reportedly sat here watching pirates being hanged at Execution Dock opposite (now moved downstream to Blackwall). The **Mayflower** pub, a 17thC inn, was renamed to commemorate the sailing of the Pilgrim Fathers' boat, the *Mayflower*, carrying pilgrims to America in 1620. It is still the only inn licensed to sell stamps to British and foreign sailors. Old warehouses and former ship-building yards line the banks as far as **101 Deptford Creek**, where the Royal Dock was built in 1513 for Henry VIII's navy. It was here Elizabeth I visited Sir Francis Drake's ship the *Golden Hind* and from here Captain

pubs including 91 the **Prospect of Whitby** dating to the reign of Henry VIII and once known as the Devil's Tavern, such were its associations with thieves and smugglers. Next door is 93 the **Town of Ramsgate** with an equally grisly past, where convicts were chained in cellars at the inn before deportation to Australia. By the pub are 92 **Wapping Old Stairs**, where Colonel Blood was caught trying to escape with the Crown Jewels. Shadwell, behind Wapping, was once densely populated with watermen, lightermen and sailors. Captain James Cook stayed here in between his three Pacific explorations. Limehouse, named after its lime kilns, was originally a ship-building centre and was where the first Chinese sailors set up their community. Later, hounded out by British seamen, they moved away and are now only remembered by a few street names (Pekin, Nankin, Canton) and restaurants. The Isle of Dogs, so called because it was once the royal kennel, was uninhabited until 1800. At the northernmost strip of these waters is 98 **Canary Wharf**, an 80-acre (35ha) development with shops, offices, apartments, restaurants, gardens and waterfront promenades. It is also home to the tallest building in the United Kingdom, One Canada

Canary Wharf Tower

Square, which stands 50 storeys high, at 800ft (244m), and dominates the skyline for miles around. The West India Docks are also the site of 99 **Billingsgate Fish Market**, which was originally based near London Bridge. Millwall (home of a notoriously rowdy football team) provides good opportunities to see smart, colourful riverside apartments next to old housing. Wherever you go, the high tracks of the Docklands Light Railway rise unexpectedly behind houses and between streets. At the tip of the Isle of Dogs, at 100 **Island Gardens**, is a pedestrian tunnel which leads under the Thames to Greenwich. From the Island Gardens side are excellent views of Wren's Royal Naval College set off by Greenwich Park. From Greenwich you can take a river trip to the Thames Barrier (see South Bank) via the vast docks (off map) Royal Victoria, Royal Albert and King George V, the last to be built (1921). With immense resources for cargo and passengers, they enjoyed prime importance, until closure in the early 1970s and later transformation into an airstrip (London City Airport) and a centre for watersports. The river here is peppered with wharfs and jetties, a reminder of the days of merchants and constant cargo deliveries.

Blackwall Tunnel
The original was built in 1897 by Sir Alexander Binnie. Now there are two tunnels, the second opened in 1967. One is used for northbound traffic and the other for southbound.

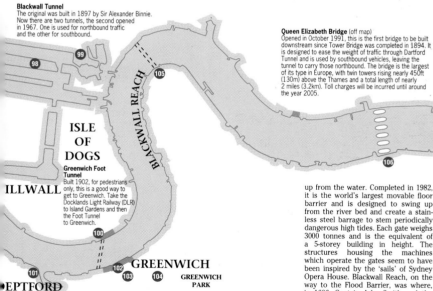

Queen Elizabeth Bridge (off map)
Opened in October 1991, this is the first bridge to be built downstream since Tower Bridge was completed in 1894. It is designed to ease the weight of traffic through Dartford Tunnel and is used by southbound vehicles, leaving the tunnel to carry those northbound. The bridge is the largest of its type in Europe, with twin towers rising nearly 450ft (130m) above the Thames and a total length of nearly 2 miles (3.2km). Toll charges will be incurred until around the year 2005.

ISLE
OF
DOGS

BLACKWALL REACH

Greenwich Foot Tunnel
Built 1902, for pedestrians only, this is a good way to get to Greenwich. Take the Docklands Light Railway (DLR) to Island Gardens and then the Foot Tunnel to Greenwich.

ILLWALL

GREENWICH

GREENWICH
PARK

EPTFORD

up from the water. Completed in 1982, it is the world's largest movable floor barrier and is designed to swing up from the river bed and create a stainless steel barrage to stem periodically dangerous high tides. Each gate weighs 3000 tonnes and is the equivalent of a 5-storey building in height. The structures housing the machines which operate the gates seem to have been inspired by the 'sails' of Sydney Opera House. Blackwall Reach, on the way to the Flood Barrier, was where, in 1606, Captain John Smith and the Virginia Settlers left on their journey to found the first permanent colony in America. Here also the *Cutty Sark* unloaded her valuable cargoes. 105 **Execution Dock** is at the entrance to Blackwall Tunnel. This is where, until the late 19thC, the bodies of convicted pirates were hung in iron cages until three tides had washed over them. A warning to all passing sailors!

Cook's *Discovery* set sail. Deptford is still used by some big cargo ships. Greenwich is rich in nautical history. Here, in dry dock, are the *Cutty Sark*, the only surviving tea-clipper, and Sir Francis Chichester's tiny ketch *Gipsy Moth IV*. Right by Greenwich Pier is Sir Christopher Wren's beautiful baroque building, 102 the **Royal Naval College**, which will be auctioned during 1996. Behind it are 103 The **National Maritime Museum** and, on its hilltop setting within Greenwich Park, 104 the **Old Royal Observatory**, home of the Greenwich Meridian. From here it is a short boatride to 106 the **Thames Flood Barrier**, best seen from the river. Rounding the bend, the steel fins rise

*O*utdoor London

London has over 80 parks within 7 miles of its centre, more than any other city in the world. They are all that remain of early London's surrounding countryside. Each park has an individual character ranging from the heathland of Hampstead to the peaceful lawns and gardens of Holland Park. All parks are free to enter, but there may be charges to use the facilities within.

PARKS, GARDENS & ZOOS

Battersea Park SW11   **103 G6**
Albert Bridge Rd 0181-871 7530. Opened in 1853 by Queen Victoria. Many original features of this 200-acre park still exist such as the Ornamental Lake and a variety of formal gardens. In 1951 the Festival Pleasure Gardens were laid out to celebrate the Festival of Britain. The magnificent Peace Pagoda, completed in 1985, was built by the Japanese Buddhist order Nipponzan Myohoji. The park is also host to the Easter Show and fair. *Open dawn-dusk Mon-Sun.*

Chelsea Physic Garden   **102 C5**
Royal Hospital Rd SW3. 0171-352 5646. Founded in 1673 by the Worshipful Society of Apothecaries, for the collection and study of plants with medicinal value. Seeds and plants have been exchanged world-wide since 1683 and botanical research is still carried out here. In the gardens is the oldest 'purpose-built' rockery, which was made from Icelandic lava and old stone from the Tower of London. Also many fine trees. *Open Apr-Oct 14.00-17.00 Wed, 14.00-18.00 Sun; 12.00-17.00 Mon-Fri during Chelsea Flower Show and Chelsea Festival weeks. Other times by appointment only.* Charge.

Green Park   **93 H3**
SW1. 0171-930 1793. Green Park is just that – no statues, lakes or flower beds, just 53 acres (22ha) of grass and trees in the centre of London. A favourite for nearby office workers at *lunchtime in summer. Open dawn-dusk Mon-Sun.*

Greenwich Park
SE10. 0181-858 2608. A royal park used by Henry VIII, whose favourite residence was nearby Greenwich Palace (the Royal Naval College now occupies the site). 200 acres (81ha) of parkland with avenues lined with chestnut trees sloping down to the Thames,

and 13 acres (5ha) of wooded deer park. Panoramic views from Greenwich Hill. The National Maritime Museum (see page 19) and the Old Royal Observatory (see page 4) are within the park. *Open Apr-Oct 05.00 (for pedestrians – 07.00 for traffic)-22.00 Mon-Sun; Nov-Mar 07.00-18.00 (or dusk) Mon-Sun.*

Hampstead Heath
(including Kenwood, Golders Hill Park, Parliament Hill) NW3. 0181-348 9930/455 5183. Open and hilly with a feel of real countryside, this is 800 acres (324ha) of park and woodland with fine views of London. Crowded on *Bank hols* with visitors to the famous fair and equally famous pubs, the Bull & Bush, Spaniard's Inn and Jack Straw's Castle. Open-air concerts at Kenwood in *summer.* Golders Hill Park has a children's zoo, playground and a fine English town garden. Parliament Hill is a good spot for kite-flying. *Open 24 hrs Mon-Sun.* Kenwood and Golders Hill Park *closed at night.*

Holland Park   **89 G3**
W8. 0171-602 9483. A haven of tranquillity from the bustle of Kensington High Street, the park has 55 acres (22ha) of calm and secluded lawns and gardens with peacocks, peafowl and pheasants. Once the private garden of Holland House, the Dutch garden dates from 1812 with fine bedding displays. Also iris and rose gardens, a yucca lawn, Japanese garden and the Orangery in which, during *May-Sep,* craft fairs, art exhibitions and other events are held. On the north side there is remarkable woodland of 28 acres (11ha) containing 3000 species of rare British trees and plants. Open-air theatre in *summer* (see page 56). *Open 07.30-dusk.* Flower garden illuminated at night and can be seen from the restaurant *open to 24.00.*

Hyde Park   **92 B1**
W1. 0171-298 2100. A royal park since 1536, it was once part of the forest reserved by Henry VIII for hunting wild boar and bulls. It became the haunt of highwaymen until 1750 and even today is patrolled at night by police. Hyde Park has 360 acres (138ha) of parkland, walks, Rotten Row for horse-riders, and the Serpentine – a fine lake, created originally from six ponds. The Serpentine Bridge is by George Rennie, 1826. The famous Speakers' Corner, a tribute to British democracy, is near Marble Arch. Baseball and soft-

ball are often played in the summer. Open-air bar and restaurant overlooking the lake. *Open 05.00-24.00 Mon-Sun.* The Lido *open May-Sep & Bank hols 10.00-18.00.* Charge for swimming and boating.

Kensington Gardens   **91 G2**
W8. 0171-298 2117. A formal and elegant addition to Hyde Park exuding genteel charm. 275 acres (111ha) of royal park, containing William III's delightful Kensington Palace, Queen Anne's Orangery, the peaceful 'Sunken Garden' and the Round Pond. The famous Broad Walk, originally flanked by ancient elms, is now replanted with fragrant limes and maples and the nearby 'Flower Walk' is home to many birds. Queen Caroline created both the Long Water (where you can see the statue of Peter Pan) and the Serpentine by ordering the damming of the Westbourne river. Nothing so rowdy as cars or football are allowed! Café. *Open dawn-dusk Mon-Sun.*

Kew Gardens
Kew Rd, Richmond, Surrey. 0181-940 1171. The Royal Botanic Gardens at Kew were founded in 1759 by Princess Augusta. Bound by the River Thames on one side and stocked with thousands of flowers and trees. Within the 300-acre (121ha) grounds are many fascinating hot-houses for orchids, palms, ferns, cacti and alpine plants. The lake, aquatic garden and 10-storey pagoda were designed by Sir William Chambers in 1760 and the magnificent curved glass Palm House and Temperate House, 1884-8, are by Decimus Burton. The botanical study was developed by its two directors Sir William and Sir Joseph Hooker. Beneath the Palm House is a Marine Display of algae and coral reefs. The Princess of Wales Conservatory contains several different climactic zones. A new Evolution House focuses on the first plants on Earth. Café and gift shop in the Orangery. Hot-houses *open 09.30-16.00.* Gardens *open from 09.30, closing times vary according to season.* Charge.

London Zoo and Aquarium   **71 E1**
Regent's Park NW1. 0171-722 3333. This famous zoo has one of the largest collections of animals in the world and is developing a strong conservation role. Aviary designed by Lord Snowdon and 'Moonlight World' where day and night are reversed and rarely seen nocturnal animals are kept awake during the day. Aquarium has fine seafish, octopuses and sting-rays. Restaurant. Café. *Open Apr-Oct 10.00-17.30 Mon-Sun; Nov-Mar 10.00-16.00 Mon-Sun.* Charge.

Regent's Park   **71 E3**
NW1. 0171-486 7905. A royal park of 472 acres (191ha), it was originally part of Henry VIII's great hunting forest in the 16thC. In 1811, the Prince Regent planned to connect the park via the newly built Regent Street to Carlton House. Although never fully completed, the design (1812-26) by John Nash is of great distinction. It forms two concentric circles – the Inner with gardens and Outer with Regency terraces and imposing gateways. Here you'll find London Zoo, the Regent's Canal, a fine boating lake with 30 species of bird, a bandstand, fragrant flower gardens and the very fine Queen Mary's Rose Garden. It is also home to the golden-domed London Mosque (see page 10). Open-air theatre (see page 56), restaurant and cafés. *Open 05.00 (or dawn)-dusk Mon-Sun.*

Primrose Hill
NW1. 0171-486 7905. 112 acres (46ha) of open land, north of Regent's Park across the canal. At 206ft (62m) the views over London are excellent and there is a helpful table identifying some of the most prominent landmarks. Popular with duellists in the 19thC, the cleverest battles you'll see now are between kite flyers. *Open 24 hrs Mon-Sun.*

Richmond Park
Surrey. 0181-948 3209. The largest of the royal parks, created by Charles I in 1637 – it covers 2358 acres (954ha). Once home to the old Palace of Shene, all that remains is the gateway bearing the arms of Henry VII. Retains all the qualities of a great English feudal estate – a natural open park of spinneys and plantations, bracken and ancient oaks (survivors of the great oak forests of the Middle Ages) and over 600 red and fallow deer. Badgers, weasels and the occasional fox can be seen. Pen Ponds are well stocked with fish (permit required). There are fine views of the Thames Valley from White Lodge (once a royal residence, now home to the Royal Ballet School). Restaurant and café in Pembroke Lodge. *Open 07.00-$\frac{1}{2}$ hr before dusk (from 07.30 in winter) Mon-Sun.*

St James's Park   **94 C3**
SW1. 0171-930 1793. St James's is the oldest royal park, acquired by Henry VIII in 1532 and laid out in imitation 'Versailles' style by Charles II. In the 1820s it was redesigned for George IV by John Nash. It is a most attractive park, with fine promenades and walks, and a romantic Chinese-style lake, bridge, and weeping willows. The bird sanctuary on Duck Island has some magnificent pelicans and over 20 species of duck and goose. Good views of Buckingham Palace, the grand sweep of Carlton House Terrace, the domes and spires of Whitehall and, to the south, Westminster Abbey. The Mall and Constitution Hill are frequently part of ceremonial and royal occasions. *Open dawn-24.00 Mon-Sun.*

Karl Marx, Highgate Cemetery

CEMETERIES

London's cemeteries provide a fascinating insight into Victorian attitudes, with their impressive and often idiosyncratic monuments. Many were created during the 19thC as a solution to overcrowded churchyards and the threat of cholera. They were originally privately owned and regimentally planted out with trees and flowers. Since then, several have become overgrown and peaceful sanctuaries for wildlife.

Brompton   **100 C5**
Old Brompton Rd SW10. Behind the busy Fulham Road, Brompton Cemetery is vast and full of ornamental Victorian marble tombs and memorials. The main entrance is surrounded by a triumphal arch. Emmeline Pankhurst, the suffragette, was buried here in 1928.

Highgate
Swain's Lane, Highgate N6. 0181-340 1834 (Friends of Highgate Cemetery). Popular ever since its opening in 1839 as a final resting place because of the good views of London from Highgate West Hill! Winding paths amongst mature trees lead up to The Egyptian Avenue and Cedar of Lebanon. Amongst its famous residents are the writer George Eliot, Karl Marx, the actor Sir Ralph Richardson, the poet Christina Rossetti and the architect himself, Stephen Geary. Tom Sayers, the bare fisted prizefighter, is guarded by the effigy of his mastiff who was chief mourner at his funeral and attended the ceremony in his own carriage. The native woodland and abundance of wild flowers and birds are conserved by the Friends of Highgate Cemetery, who offer guided tours round the western section *Apr-Oct at 12.00, 14.00 & 16.00 Mon-Fri, on the hour 11.00-16.00 Sat & Sun; Nov & Mar at 12.00, 14.00 & 15.00 Mon-Fri, on the hour 11.00-15.00 Sat & Sun.* Eastern section *open Apr-Oct 10.00-17.00 Mon-Fri, 11.00-17.00 Sat & Sun; Nov-Mar 10.00-16.00 Mon-Fri, 11.00-16.00 Sat & Sun. Closed during funerals.* Charge.

Kensal Green
Harrow Rd, Kensal Green W10. 0181-969 0152. This was the first of the great commercial cemeteries in London. It became a fashionable place to be buried after the royal burials of two of George III's children, the Duke of Sussex and Princess Sophia. There are plenty of monuments to admire and many mature native trees lining the curving avenues. Other famous tombs include W.M. Thackeray and Anthony Trollope, Isambard Kingdom Brunel and his father Sir Marc Isambard Brunel. *Open 09.00-17.00 Mon-Sat, 10.00-17.30 Sun (earlier closing in winter).* Guided tours by the Friends of Kensal Green Cemetery *Mar-Sep at 14.30 Sat & Sun; Oct-Feb at 14.00 Sun.* Donations requested.

Shopping

SHOPPING AREAS

Covent Garden   83 F5
Once the site of the famous fruit and vegetable market, this refurbished area is now a fashionable pedestrianised piazza. The arcades are lined with small specialist fashion and gift shops, plus plenty of places to eat and drink. Open-air craft stalls, an antiques market and an occasional craft market. Leading off the piazza in every direction, the streets reveal an interesting variety of shops and restaurants with the latest in fashion, high-tech household equipment and exotic foods. *Late night Thur, but many shops are open late every night and on Sundays.*

Kensington High Street   90 C4
Less hectic than Oxford Street, though a similar range of shops and large branches of most high street chains, plus Barkers of Kensington, its own department store. Delve into the roads leading off for more individual (and more expensive) fashion shops. *Late night Thur.*

King's Road/Chelsea   102 C3
Still as much a place to be seen in as to see, this area really comes alive on *Sat.* One of the centres for up-to-the-minute fashion, plus high street chains. Particularly good for shoes and men's clothing. *Late night Wed.*

Knightsbridge   92 C4
A traditionally fashionable area for the rich and famous, dominated by Harrods and Harvey Nichols. Beauchamp Place has exclusive furniture, jewellery and clothes. *Late night Wed.*

Piccadilly/Trocadero/London Pavilion   82 C6
Quality and tradition in the form of Fortnum & Mason, Hatchards, Simpson, and Lillywhites. Also the historic Burlington Arcade. The Trocadero and London Pavilion cater for the more up-to-date taste with one-stop shopping, refreshment and entertainment, while Tower Records dominates Piccadilly Circus from the old Swan & Edgar building. *Many shops open late Mon-Sat.*

Soho   82 C4
Much less sleazy these days, but as cosmopolitan as ever, Soho is excellent for specialist shopping. International food shops, oriental supermarkets, and designer clothes. Also trendy bars and restaurants. Berwick Street Market and Chinatown are both worth a visit.

Gerrard Street, Chinatown

West End

London's biggest shopping area consisting of three main streets. *Oxford Street* (82 B3) is over a mile long and has nearly all the major department stores including Selfridges, John Lewis, London's largest Marks & Spencer and an overwhelming assortment of individual fashion shops. Very crowded, especially on *Sat* and at *lunchtime*. *Regent Street* (82 A5) is less hectic and offers luxurious items and gifts at Liberty, plus several china, glass and clothing stores and the fashion and beauty department store Dickins & Jones. *Carnaby Street* (82 A4) which was world-renowned in the 1960s, has retained its busy and lively atmosphere, with frequent pavement shows and interesting clothes and souvenir shops. For real luxury try *New Bond Street* (81 H5) where you'll find shoes, jewellery, prints, pictures and designer clothes. Two pedestrianised streets just off Oxford Street, and well worth exploring, are *St Christopher's Place* (81 F4) and *South Molton Street* (81 G4). Both are packed with stylish small shops and attractive eating places. *Late night Thur.*

Whiteleys   78 D6
Queensway W2. 0171-229 8844. One of the first department stores, now transformed into a cosmopolitan complex of shops, cafés, restaurants, bars and an eight-screen cinema, UCI Whiteleys. Centre *open to 24.00 Mon-Sun,* but most shops *open to 20.00 Mon-Sat.*

Fortnum & Mason

DEPARTMENT STORES

Barkers of Kensington   90 C4
63 Kensington High St W8. 0171-937 5432. Clothes, household and electrical goods.

BHS   81 H4
252 Oxford St W1. 0171-629 2011. Inexpensive clothes and household goods. Excellent lighting department.

Debenhams   81 G4
344-348 Oxford St W1. 0171-580 3000. Fashion clothing, kitchenware, lingerie, hosiery and cosmetics.

D.H. Evans   81 G4
318 Oxford St W1. 0171-629 8800. Excellent fashion and lingerie departments. Also perfumery, furniture and household goods. Olympus Sports in the basement.

Dickins & Jones   82 A4
224 Regent St W1. 0171-734 7070. Stylish ladies' and men's clothing, accessories and haberdashery. Also china and glass.

Fortnum & Mason   94 B1
181 Piccadilly W1. 0171-734 8040. Well-respected store established in 1760. Particularly famous for its exotic foods and provisions, but also has jewellery, china and glass, designer clothes, perfumery, leather goods, toys and stationery.

Harrods   92 C5
Knightsbridge SW1. 0171-730 1234. The world's most famous department store established in 1849 by a tea merchant, Henry Harrod. There are over 60 fashion departments with men's, ladies' and children's clothing, perfumes, accessories, gifts, china, glass, pets, toys, books, furniture and fabrics. The Edwardian marble Food Halls offer luxury foods.

Harvey Nichols   92 D4
109-125 Knightsbridge SW1. 0171-235 5000. Elegant, stylish clothes from top designers. Accessories, home furnishings and a Food Hall. *Open 10.00-19.00 Mon-Fri (to 20.00 Wed), to 18.00 Sat.*

John Lewis   81 H4
278-306 Oxford St W1. 0171-629 7711. Large dress fabric department, furniture, furnishings, china, glass, household goods, haberdashery and fashions. No credit cards.

Liberty   82 A4
210-220 Regent St W1. 0171-734 1234. Famous for its distinctive fabrics and unusual luxury goods. Jewellery, gifts, glass, china, rugs, prints, designer-label fashions.

Marks & Spencer   81 E5
458 Oxford St W1. 0171-935 7954. Well-loved chain of stores with good quality, inexpensive clothing. Also home furnishings,

raincoats for men and women cut in the English style. Hats, scarves, suits and accessories. Other branches.

Lillywhites 82 C6
Piccadilly Circus W1. 0171-930 3181. Five floors of sports clothing and equipment for just about any sport you can think of.

Simpson 82 B6
203 Piccadilly W1. 0171-734 2002. High-quality clothing. Daks country clothing, Squadron sportswear, luggage and accessories.

SPECIALIST SHOPS

ANTIQUES

Antiquarius 101 G6
137 King's Rd SW3. Market with 150 stalls selling antique clothing, jewellery, china, glass, books and prints.

Chelsea Antiques Market 102 A5
245-253 King's Rd SW3. 0171-352 5581. Large, busy market – period clothing, watches, books, prints and scientific instruments.

Grays Antiques Market 81 G5
1-7 Davies Mews W1. 0171-629 7034. Two huge Victorian warehouses with wide selection of antiques – luggage, leather goods, toys, games and jewellery.

AUCTIONEERS

W. & F.C. Bonham & Sons 92 B4
Montpelier Galleries, Montpelier St SW7. 0171-584 9161. Paintings, furniture, carpets, porcelain, jewellery and silver.

Christie's 94 B2
8 King St SW1. 0171-839 9060. Internationally famous. Comprehensive fine art auctioneers since 1766. Free estimates.

Sotheby's 81 H5
34-35 New Bond St W1. 0171-493 8080. Internationally famous for antiques and works of art. Paintings, ceramics, glass, furniture, silver, jewellery, books and manuscripts.

BOOKS

Dillons 102 B3
150-152 King's Rd SW3. 0171-351 2023. Vast stock of paperbacks and hardbacks. *Open 09.00-21.00 Mon & Wed-Sat, 09.30-21.00 Tue, 12.00-18.00 Sun.* Other branches.

Foyles 82 D4
119-125 Charing Cross Rd WC2. 0171-437 5660. London's largest book store with practically every English book in print.

Hatchards 94 B2
187 Piccadilly W1. 0171-439 9921. A comprehensive selection of general books and knowledgeable staff.

Harrods

cosmetics, gifts and excellent Food Hall. No credit cards. *Open 09.00-19.00 Mon-Wed & Sat, to 20.00 Thur & Fri, 12.00-18.00 Sun.*

Peter Jones 102 D2
Sloane Sq SW1. 0171-730 3434. Excellent quality and value clothing, accessories, household goods, furniture, glass, china, fabrics. No credit cards.

Selfridges 81 F4
400 Oxford St W1. 0171-629 1234. Vast store with a huge range of clothing, accessories and household goods, toys, sports clothing and equipment and an impressive Food Hall.

CLOTHES STORES

Nearly all London's department stores have extensive clothing collections. These are the specialists:

Aquascutum 82 B6
100 Regent St W1. 0171-734 6090. Fine quality British raincoats, coats, suits, knitwear and accessories.

Austin Reed 82 B6
103 Regent St W1. 0171-734 6789. English and Continental suits and accessories for men with the accent on quality. Also ladies' clothing, executive suits and designer wear.

Burberrys 82 C6
18 Haymarket SW1. 0171-930 3343. Classic

W.H. Smith   **102 D3**
36 Sloane Sq SW1. 0171-730 0351. Well-known retailer, with a wide choice of books, magazines, stationery, records, tapes, CDs and games. Many other branches.

Waterstone's   **90 B5**
193 Kensington High St W8. 0171-937 8432. Excellent general store with comprehensive selections in just about every subject you can think of. *Open 09.30-21.00 Mon-Fri, to 19.00 Sat, 12.00-18.00 Sun.* Other branches.

CRAFTS AND GIFTS

Covent Garden General Store   **83 E5**
111 Long Acre WC2. 0171-240 2058. Two floors with sections representing various companies. Large range of gifts, ornaments and clothing. *Open 10.00-20.00 Mon-Sun (to 22.30 Sat).*

Crabtree & Evelyn   **90 C3**
6 Kensington Church St W8. 0171-937 9335. Exquisite perfumes and toiletries – all beautifully packaged. Other branches.

General Trading Company   **102 D1**
144 Sloane St SW1. 0171-730 0411. Some of the best designs in contemporary English and Continental glass and china. Good café.

Givans Irish Linen Stores   **102 B4**
207 King's Rd SW3. 0171-352 6352. Top-quality linen from a store with an air of old-fashioned gentility. *Closed Sat.*

Past Times   **92 B5**
146 Brompton Rd SW3. 0171-581 7616. Reproduction jewellery, crafts and cards from 4000 years of British history. Other branches.

TOYS

Hamleys
188-196 Regent St W1. 0171-734 3161. Largest toy shop in London – six floors of it. Has nearly every toy and game you can think of. *Open 10.00-19.00 Mon-Fri (to 20.00 Thur), 09.30-19.00 Sat, 12.00-18.00 Sun.*

MARKETS

Berwick Street Market   **82 B3**
W1. Busy and boisterous general market in the heart of Soho. Good value fruit and vegetables; also meat, cheeses, fresh fish and household goods. *Open 09.00-18.00 Mon-Sat.*

Camden Lock Market
Where Chalk Farm Rd crosses Regent's Canal NW1. Among the cobbled courtyards and warehouses of the lock is a huge market area

selling everything from designer clothes and antique furniture to junk. Interesting food stalls. Market *open 10.00-18.00 Mon-Sat, 09.30-17.30 Sun.*

Petticoat Lane Market   **86 B2**
The name given to the market radiating from Middlesex Street. Probably named after the second-hand clothes dealers who had their businesses here in the early 1600s. Lively and hectic, with mainly clothing on sale, but also toys, food, toiletries and luxury goods. *Open 09.00-14.00 Sun only.*

Portobello Road Market   **77 G3**
W11. Well-known and much-frequented market extending into Golborne Road and Westbourne Grove. Fruit, vegetables and new goods sold *09.00-18.00 Mon-Wed, to 13.00 Thur.* Second-hand junk and bric-à-brac sold *08.00-17.00 Fri,* and the famous antiques market is held *08.00-sunset Sat.*

AFTERNOON TEA

Most large department stores such as *Fortnum & Mason, Selfridges, Harrods* and *Harvey Nichols* serve excellent afternoon tea in their restaurants. However, if you want to avoid the hustle and bustle of busy shopping areas, the following hotels and pâtisseries are among the best:

Brown's Hotel   **82 A6**
Dover St W1. 0171-493 6020. In an English country house setting, Brown's is an excellent choice for afternoon tea. Sandwiches, cakes, muffins. *Served 15.00-18.00.*

Claridges   **81 G5**
Brook St W1. 0171-629 8860. A touch of class in the reading room, where liveried footmen serve sandwiches and pastries. *Served 15.00-17.30 (Reserve).*

Pâtisserie Valerie   **83 D4**
44 Old Compton St W1. 0171-437 3466. Long-established Soho pâtisserie. Tea, coffee and hot chocolate accompany superb cakes and sandwiches. *Served all day Mon-Sun.* Other branches.

Ritz Hotel   **94 A1**
Piccadilly W1. 0171-493 8181. Tea in the Palm Court, with dainty sandwiches, pastries and cream cakes. *Served 15.00 & 16.30 (Reserve Sat & Sun).*

Waldorf Hotel   **83 G4**
Aldwych WC2. 0171-836 2400. Opulent Palm Court tea lounge with comfort and good service. Tea served *15.30-18.30 daily.* London's most famous tea dance *Sat & Sun (Reserve).*

Oxford Street

Tottenham Court Road	
Fashion M **Hornes**	4
Pub **The Tottenham**	6
Restaurant **McDonald's**	8
Sock Shop	10
CDs, records & cassettes **Virgin Megastore**	14
Foodstore **7-Eleven**	24
Lloyds Bank	32
Shoes FM **Barratts**	36
Leather goods **Shot**	38
Fashion FM **Academy**	44
Leather goods **Eternité**	46
Restaurant **Angus Steak House**	48
Hanway Street	
Take-away food **Benjy's**	50
Midland Bank	52
Rathbone Place	
Restaurant **Prêt à Manger**	56
Fashion FM **Harley-Davidson**	58
Building society Halifax	60
Natural beauty products **The Body Shop**	66
Travel goods **Salisburys**	68a
Perry's Place	
Hi-fi **McDonalds Electronics**	70
Shoes FM **Shoe Express**	74
Newsagent, gifts & cards **Oxford News**	78
CDs **Buzzz**	80
Shoes FM **Dolcis**	82
Cameras & electronics **Dixons**	86

Newman Street	
Opticians **Eyeland – Dolland & Aitchison**	92
Chemist **Boots**	94
Zone Games Centre	100
Nightclub **100 Club**	100
Gifts **Angelic**	112
National Westminster Bank	112

Berners Street	
Fashion F **Principles**	114
Fashion M **High & Mighty**	116
Fashion FM **Tie Rack**	118
SHOPPING CENTRE THE PLAZA	
Coffee & tea **Whittard**	122a
Accessories **Accessorize**	122
Fashion FM **The Gap**	124

Wells Street	
Camping equipment **Millets**	134
Fashion M **The Suit Company**	134
Fashion M **Mister Byrite**	140
Restaurant **Burger King**	142
Novelties, cards **Surprise**	146
Records **HMV Shop**	150
Fashion M **Oakland**	156
Fashion FM **California Jeans**	158
Fashion M **Profile**	160
Fashion M **The State of Independence**	162

Winsley Street	
Fashion M **Blazer**	170
Sportswear **Cobra**	172
Baby store **Mothercare**	174
Fashion FM **Mark-One**	178

Great Titchfield Street	
Shoes FM **Ravel**	184
Sock Shop	190
Shoes FM **Faith**	192
Midland Bank	196
STORE **C&A**	202

Charing Cross Road	
7	**Morgan** *Fashion F*
⊖	Tottenham Court Road
15	**Clark's** *Shoes FM*
17	**Wigwam** *Gifts & leather goods*
19	Regent School of Languages
19	Challoner *Employment agency*
19	**Dillons** *Books*
25	Office Angels *Employment agency*
25	**Messrs C** *Foods*
27	**Tepee** *Fashion FM*
29	**Pizza Hut** *Restaurant*
33	**Nick Nack** *Fashion M*
35	**Papagallo's** *Take-away food*
37	**Ryman** *Stationery*
41	**Cardshops** *Cards & posters*
43	**Connan** *Fashion FM*
43	**Chequepoint** *Bureau de Change*
45	**Sightcare** *Opticians*
45	Mayfair School of English
47	Key *Employment agency*
47	**Sonico Jeans Centre** *Fashion FM*
49	**Outlet 49** *Fashion F*
49	Kelly *Employment agency*
51	**The Bootstore**
53	**Mondo Pelle** *Leather fashion*
55	**Suits You** *Fashion M*
Soho Street	
63	Chequepoint *Bureau de change*
65	**Play to Win** *Amusement Arcade*
71	**Tribe** *Fashion FM*
73	**Mash** *Fashion M*
77	**Madhouse** *Fashion FM*
79	**79 Club** *Nightclub*
83	**Toro Leather Wear** *Fashion FM*
85	**Marmalade** *Fashion M*
87	**Pizza Hut** *Restaurant*
89	**Sock Shop**
Dean Street	
91	**Tie Rack** *Fashion FM*
93	**Knickerbox** *Underwear*
95	**Eurochange** *Bureau de change*
97	**Woodhouse** *Fashion M*
101	**Crest** *Souvenirs*

Great Chapel Street	
103	**Slot Machine** *Fashion FM*
105	**Silverdale** *Travel goods*
109	**Mark-One** *Fashion F*
111	**Cobra** *Sports goods*
113	**Mister Pound** *Discount store*
115	**Warrior** *Fashion M*
117	**Benny Dee** *Discount lingerie*
123	**Holland & Barrett** *Health foodstore*
125	**Benetton** *Fashion F*

Wardour Street	
127a	**Hard Ruck** *Travel goods*
127	**Corenby Ltd Co** *Tax-free clearance*
129	**Clearance Depot** *Clearance store*
129	**Dimensions** *Hair studio*
135	**Bradforce Ltd** *Tax-free goods*
137	**Footsie 100** *Shoes FM*
139	Callan School of English

Berwick Street	
145	**J. D. Sports** *Sportswear*
145	**DIS School of Computing**
145	Accountants on Call *Employment agency*
147	**Sacha** *Shoes FM*
149	**Jeans West** *Fashion FM*
151	**Boots** *Chemist*
153	**Jane Norman** *Fashion F*
155	**The Sale** *Fashion FM*
159	**Shellys** *Shoes FM*

Poland Street	
163	**Books Etc** *Books*
165	Abbey National *Building society*
167	**H.Samuel** *Jewellers*
173	**MARKS & SPENCER** *STORE*
175	**Saxone** *Shoes FM*
181	Next *Employment agency*
181	**Dolcis** *Shoes FM*
185	Ecco *Recruitment consultants*
185	**McDonald's** *Restaurant*
187	**Bankrupt Clothing Co** *Fashion FM*
189	**Next** *Fashion FM*

Ramilles Street	
199	**Leslie Davis** *Jewellers*
201	**Paperchase** *Gifts*
213	**LITTLEWOODS** *STORE*
217	**Wallis** *Fashion F*
219	**Knickerbox** *Underwear*

Oxford Street continued

Great Portland Street			***Hills Place***
Restaurant **Burger King**	214	221	**Miss Selfridge** Fashion F
Fashion F **Anne Brooks** (Petite Fashion)	216	225	**The Vestry** Fashion F
Fashion F **Evans**	218	227	**Crest of London** Souvenirs
		229	**Gipsy** Fashion FM
		231	**Jeans West** Fashion FM
		233	**The Byrite Company** Fashion M
		235	Thomas Cook Bureau de change
			Argyll Street
STORE **TOP SHOP & TOP MAN**	220-226	241	Exchange International Bureau de change
		245	**Shellys** Shoes FM
Oxford Circus	⊖		***Regent Street***
Fashion F **Hennes**	238	257	**Sock Shop**
John Prince's Street		261	**For Eyes** Opticians
		263	**Richards** Fashion F
Fashion M **Mister Byrite**	244	267	**J. D. Sports** Sportswear
Shoes FM **Bally**	246	271	**La Baguette Parisienne** Take-away food
Shoes FM **Ravel**	248	273	**Scottish Woollens** Fashion, knitwear
Jewellers **H. Samuel**	250	275	Salvation Army Hall
STORE **BHS**	252	277	**Ernest Jones** Jewellers
Shoes FM **Clarks**	260	283	**River Island** Fashion FM
Fashion F **Jane Norman**	262	285	**Boots** Chemist
Fashion F **Monsoon**	264	287	**Cecil Gee** Fashion M
Fashion F **Ann Harvey**	266	289	**The Deep Pan Pizza Co** Restaurant
Natural beauty products **The Body Shop**	268	291	Bureau de change
Greetings cards **Clinton**	270	291	**Mr Howard** Fashion M
Fashion F **Wallis**	272	291	**Shirts, Ties & Sock Shop** Fashion FM
		291b	**McDonald's** Restaurant
Holles Street			***Harewood Place***
STORE **JOHN LEWIS**	273-306	293	**Accessorize** Accessories
		295	**Tie Rack** Fashion FM
		297	**Saxone** Shoes FM
		299	**Babers** Shoes M
		299	**Blue Arrow** Employment agency
		301	**Olympus Sports** Sports goods and sportswear
		305	**Tesco Metro** Foodstore
		309	**Swatch** Watches
		315	Acme Employment agency
Old Cavendish Street		315	**The Gap** Fashion FM, childrenswear
STORE **D.H. EVANS**	318		
Chapel Place			***Dering Street***
Shoes FM **K Shoes**	324	321	**Stefanel** Fashion FM
Sock Shop	326	321	Berlitz School of Languages
Fashion FM **Naf Naf**	328	321	**Next** Fashion M
Smokers' materials **Peterson**	330	325	**Next** Fashion F
Citibank	332		
Vere Street			***New Bond Street***
STORE **DEBENHAMS**	344-348	333	**Dolcis** Shoes FM
		335	**Splash** Souvenirs
		337	**Bonjour Paris** Take-away food
		339	Bureau de change
		341	**Café Zeynah** Take-away food
		349	**Wendy's** Restaurant
Marylebone Lane			***Woodstock Street***
Ties, shirts **Off The Cuff**	350		
Telephones **British Telecom Shop**	350	353	**Thorntons** Chocolates
TSB Bank	350	353	Brook Street Employment agency
		355	**House of Cashmere** Fashion FM
Marylebone Lane		357	**Selection** Fashion FM
Souvenirs **Crest of London**	354		
Fashion FM **Art of Silk**	356		***Sedley Place***
Accessories **Sunglass Hut**	357	359	**Churchill** Gifts
National Westminster Bank	358	361	**Oakland** Fashion M
		363	**HMV Shop** Records, CDs & cassettes
		369	**La Brioche Dorée** Take-away food
		369a	Foreign Exchange Corporation
		⊖	Bond Street
		373	**Leslie Davis** Jewellers
Stratford Place			***Davies Street (South Molton Street)***
Shoes FM **Lilley & Skinner**	360	379	**Burtons/Dorothy Perkins** Fashion FM
Fashion F **Kookai**	362	379	WEST ONE SHOPPING CENTRE
Fashion M **Woodhouse**	364	383	**Oxford's** Fashion F
Jewellers **H. Samuel**	366	385	**Boots** Chemist
		393	**Jeans West** Fashion FM
St Christopher's Place		395	**The Gap** Fashion FM
Shoes FM **Bally**	368		
Fashion M **Suits You**	370		
Natural beauty products **The Body Shop**	372		
James Street			***Gilbert Street***
STORE **C&A**	376	399	**Pizzaland** Restaurant
		399	Lloyds Bank
Bird Street			***Binney Street***
Shoes FM **Instep Sports**	386	407	**Carphone Warehouse** Telephones
Fashion F **Jane Norman**	388	409	**Bertie** Shoes FM
Shoes FM **Barratts**	388	409	**Switch** Fashion F
		411	Kelly Temporary services Employment agency
		413	**Mappin & Webb** Jewellers

Oxford Street continued

	Duke Street			**Duke Street**
			415	**Ciro Citterio** Fashion M
			419	**Principles** Fashion FM
				Lumley Street
			425	**The Oxford Street General Store** Gifts
			427	**Samuel Maynard** China & gifts
			429	**Burger King** Restaurant
STORE **SELFRIDGES**		400		**Balderton Street**
			431	Midland Bank
			435	**Sock Shop**
			439	**Boots** Chemist
			443	British Nursing Association
			443	**Churchill** Gifts
			445	**London House** Fashion FM
			449	**Jean Jeanie** Fashion FM
			451	**Laura Ashley** Fashion F
	Orchard Street			**North Audley Street**
STORE **MARKS & SPENCER**		458	455	**American Burger** Restaurant
Shoes FM **Bally**		468	461	**Mothercare** Baby store
Jewellers **H. Samuel**		474	467	**House of Scotland** Fashion FM
Shoes FM **Clarks**		476	469	**Knickerbox** Underwear
Fashion F **Etam**		484	471	**House of Cashmere** Cashmeres
Chemist **Boots**		488	473	**The General Store** Souvenirs
Shoes FM **Russell & Bromley**		494	473	**Adams** Childrenswear
Travel goods **Baggage Company**		498	479	**Aberdeen Steak House** Restaurant
Watches of **Switzerland**		500	481	**Hennes** Fashion F
Shoes FM **Saxone**		502	483	**Oakland** Fashion M
			485	**The Highlands** Fashion FM
			487	Alfred Marks Employment agency
			487	**Tie Rack** Fashion FM
			489	**Bay Trading Co** Fashion M
			491	**Ryman** Stationery
			493	**Dixons** Cameras & electronics
	Portman Street			**Park Street**
STORE **LITTLEWOODS**		506		
Fashion FM **Benetton**		522	505	**C&A** STORE
Novelty goods **Cascade**		524	521	**Mad House** Fashion FM
Fashion F **Next**		526	523	**Pizza Hut** Restaurant
Travel goods **Salisburys**		530	527	**Virgin Records** Records, CDs & cassettes
Fashion F **Wallis**		532	533	**Cerex** Souvenirs
Fashion F **Evans**		538	535	**Crest of London** Souvenirs
			537	Bureau de change
	Old Quebec Street			**Park Lane**
Restaurant **Kentucky Fried Chicken**		542		
Bureau de change Chequepoint		548		
Marble Arch		⊖		
Bureau de change Berkeley Credit		550		
Cumberland Hotel		552		
China & glass **Chinacraft**		556		
	Great Cumberland Place			**Marble Arch**

Bond Street – new and old

	Oxford Street			**Oxford Street**
Shoes FM **Dolcis**		87	81	**Berkertex Brides** Bridalwear
Fashion F **Warehouse**		89	77	**Bellini** Fashion M
Fashion M **Blazer**		90	75	**Cerruti 1881** Fashion M
Fashion M **Cecil Gee**		92		
Shoes FM **Grant**		94		
	Blenheim Street			
Shoes F **Kurt Geiger**		95		**Dering Street**
Shoes F **Carvela**		96		
Royal Bank of Scotland		97		
Linens **Frette**		98	74a	**Clio** Shoes F
Fashion F **Betty Barclay**		99	74	**Watches of Bond Street** Jewellers
Shoes FM **Lanzoni**		100	74	**Alexander Juran** Oriental carpets
Auctioneers **Phillips**		101	74	Accountancy Personnel Employment agency
Leather goods **Proudfoot**		102	73	**Louis Feraud** Fashion F
Fashion FM **Red/Green**		103	72	**Timberland** Fashion M
Shoes F **Ivory**		104	70	**Jasons** Textiles
Fashion F **Laurel**		105	69	**Please Mum** Childrenswear
Fashion F **Cerruti**		105-6	68	**Robina** Fashion F
Fashion M **Gant**		107	66-67	**Escada** Fashion F
Fashion F **Lanvin**		108	65	**Guy Laroche** Fashion F
Sylvia Lewis Beauty Clinic		108	64	**Dixons** Cameras & electronics
Hairdressing salon **Paul Mitchell**		109		
Shoes FM **Russell & Bromley**		109		

Bond Street continued

Brook Street			**Brook Street**
Fashion FM **Emporio Armani**	110	63	**FENWICK** STORE
Bond Street Silver Galleries	111		
Shoes FM **Bally**	116		
Fashion M **Cecil Gee**	120		
Lane Fine Art	123		
Arcade **Bond Street Antiques Centre**	124		
Fashion M **Herbie Frogg**	125	51	**The White House** Linen
Photography **Wallace Heaton**	126	50	**Chappell Music Centre**
Fashion F **Jigsaw**	128	49	**Bruno Magli** Shoes FM
Midland Bank	129	47	**F. Pinet** Shoes FM
Grosvenor Street			**Maddox Street**
Fashion F, leather goods **Loewe**	130	46	**Avi Rossini** Fashion M
Fashion FM **Beale & Inman**	131	46	Ciao Travel
Shoes FM **Church's Shoes**	133	45	**Massada** Antiques
Fabrics **Simmonds**	134	45	**Cashmere Shop** Fashion FM
Fashion M **Yves Saint Laurent**	135	43	**Smython** Leather goods
Fashion F **Yves Saint Laurent**	137	39-41	**Mulberry Store** Fashion FM
		38	**Pal Zileri** Fashion M
Bloomfield Place		37	**Ermenegildo Zegna** Fashion FM
		36	**Fogal** Lace
Fashion F **Marie Claire**	138	34	**Sotheby's** Auctioneers
Silver & goldsmiths **S. J. Phillips**	139	32	**Richard Green** Paintings
Fashion FM **Zilli**	140	31	**Fior** Jewellers
Antiques **Mallett**	141	30	**Herbert Johnson** Milliner FM
Fashion M **Polo Ralph Lauren**	143	29	**Gordon Scott** Shoes FM
Antiques **Frank Partridge**	144	28	**Celine** Accessories F
Fine art dealers **Wildenstein**	147	27	**Wana Designs** Fashion FM
Fine Art Society	148	26	**Tessiers** Gold & silversmiths
Luggage **Louis Vuitton**	149	24	**Russell & Bromley** Shoes FM
Fashion F **Joan & David**	150		
Bruton Street			**Conduit Street**
Publishers Time & Life	155	23a	**Philip Landau** Fashion M
Luxury goods **Hermes**	155	23	**Moira** Antiques
Cashmeres **Ballantyne**	157	22a	**Massimo** Fashion M
Fashion F **Max Mara**	158	22	**Moira** Antiques
Fashion FM **Nicole Farhi**	159	21	**European Suit Store** Fashion M
Fashion FM **Valentino**	160	18	**Krizia** Fashion F
Paintings **John Mitchell & Son**	160		
Glass **Lalique**	162		
Shoes M **Church's Shoes**	163		
Employment agency Kelly Temporary Services	163		
Fashion FM **Savoy Tailors Guild**	164		
			Clifford Street
Grafton Street		16	**Watches of Switzerland**
Luxury accessories **Asprey**	165	15	**Patek Phillipe** Watches
Jewellers **Caroline Charles**	170	15	**Georg Jensen** Silversmiths
Jewellers **Collingwood**	171	14a	**Chopard** Luxury goods
Jewellers **Bulgari**	172	14	**Adler of Geneva** Jewellers
Fashion F **Karl Lagerfeld**	173	12	**Hennell** Silversmiths
Jewellers **Reposs & Co**	174	11	**Philip Antrobus** Jewellers
Jewellers **Cartier**	175	10	**Adele Davis** Fashion F
Shoes & leatherwear **Rossetti**	177	10a	**Anne Bloom** Jewellers
Jewellers **Dianoor**	178	9	**Ciro** Jewellers
Jewellers **Mikimoto**	179	8	**Bentley & Co** Antiques
Jewellers **Boucheron**	180	7	**Graff** Jewellers
Luxury goods, jewellers **Tiffany & Co**	25	4	**Richard Green** Art gallery
Fashion F **Chanel**	26	1	National Westminster Bank
The Royal Arcade	28		
Historical Portraits Ltd	30		**Burlington Gardens**
Fashion F **Christian Lacroix**	30		
Shoes FM **Bally**	30	24	**Salvatore Ferragamo** Shoes FM & accessories
Shoes F **Pied à Terre**	32	23a	**Joseph** Fashion F
Luxury goods **Gucci**	33	22	**Chatila** Jewellers
		19	**A. Sulka & Co** Fashion M
Stafford Street		17	**Clough** Jewellers & pawnbrokers
		17	**Tom Gilbey Waistcoat Gallery** Fashion FM
Fashion FM **Gianni Versace**	36	16	**Frost & Reed** Paintings
Fine art **Entwistle**	37	15	**Ricci Burns** Fashion F
Antiques **Deborah Gage**	38	14	**Colnaghi Galleries** Paintings
Marlborough Fine Art Gallery	39	13	**Leger Galleries** Paintings
Lloyds Bank	39	12	**Anna Molinari** Fashion F
Fine art **Noortman**	41	11	**Cesare Paciotti** Shoes F
Fine art **Thos. Agnew & Sons**	43	10a	**Swaine Adeney** Fashion M
Fine art **Thomas Gibson**	44	10	Lufthansa German Airlines
Fashion M **Alfred Dunn**	46	9	**Ginza Yamagataya** Fashion M
		7	Air Nippon Airlines
		5	**Gold Pfeil** Fashion F
		3	**Belgrave Carpet Gallery** Carpets
		2	**Kings of Sheffield** Antique silver
		1a	**F. B. Meyrowitz** Opticians
		1	**Watches of Switzerland**
Green Park ⊖			**Piccadilly**

South Molton Street

Oxford Street

Pub **Hog in the Pound Tavern**	28
Employment agency Select Appointments	28
Designer fashion FM **Browns**	23
Teas & Coffees **Whittards**	22
Bond Street Secretarial Bureau	22
Japanese jewellery **Electrum**	21
Fashion jewellery **Butler & Wilson**	20
Shoes FM **Pied à Terre**	19
Fashion F **Genny**	18
Employment agency Reed	17
Fashion M **Vertice**	16
Shoes FM **Jones**	15
Fashion F **French for Less**	14
Designer fashion F **Arte**	12
Restaurant **Grand Café**	11
Shoes F **Office**	10
Fashion F **Pied à Terre**	9
Shoes F **Senso**	6
Designer jewellery **André Bogaert**	5
Designer jewellery **Agatha**	4
Handbags & luggage **Le Sport Sac**	3
Fashion F **Romans**	1
Restaurant **The Lancers**	1
Fashion F **Ronit Zilkha**	34

35	**Foto Inn** Developing & printing
36	**Bertie** Shoes FM
37	**Leather Rat** Leather fashion FM
39	**Gigli** Fashion FM
40	**The Red Rock Café**
41	**Origin** Handbags
42	**Alma** Fashion M
43	**Saga** Japanese restaurant
44	**Astuces** Fashion F
45	**Karen Miller** Fashion F
45	ROC Recruitment Secretarial agency
45	**Karen Millen** Fashion F
46	**Widow Applebaum's** Jewish restaurant
47	**Hobbs** Fashion & shoes F
48	**Grosvenor Gallery**
48	**Cable & Co** Fashion M
49	**Skindeep** Leather fashions FM
50	**Browns Labels for Less** Fashion FM
51	**Vertice** Italian fashion FM
52	**Proibito** Fashion FM
53	**Geno Ventti** Hairdressing salon
54	**Fabrice Karel** Fashion F
54	Reed Accountancy Employment agency
55	**Oliver** Fashion M
56	**Bang & Olufson** TV & hi-fi

Globe Yard

57	**Adolfo Dominguez** Hairdressing salon
57	**Molton Brown** Hairdressing salon
59	Shane English School
60	**Office** Shoes FM
60	**Vidal Sassoon** Hairdressing salon
61	**Romeo Gigli** Fashion F
62	London Business College
64	**South Molton Drug Stores**
65	Post Office
66	**Sartine et Chocolat** Confectioner
67	**Monsoon** Fashion F
68	**Celia Loe** Fashion F
69	**Sock Shop** Hosiery

Regent Street

Fashion M **Original Levi's Store**	269
Restaurant **Garfunkel's**	265
Fashion F **Hennes**	260

Great Castle Street

220-226	**TOP SHOP & TOP MAN** STORE

Oxford Street

(⊖)

Oxford Street

Fashion FM **Benetton**	257
Fashion FM **French Connection**	249-256

266	**Shellys** Shoes FM
260	**Bally** Shoes FM
256	**Laura Ashley** Fashion F
254	**Thorntons** Chocolates
254	**Off the Cuff** Shirts M
246	National Westminster Bank

Princes Street

Chocolates **Godiva**	247
Fashion M **Reiss**	245
Fashion FM **House of Scotland**	241
Beauty products & comestibles **Crabtree & Evelyn**	239
Cameras & film **City Photo**	239
Underwear **Damart Thermawear**	235
Fashion FM **London House**	231
Opticians **Dollond & Aitchison**	229

Little Argyll Street

244	**DICKINS & JONES** STORE

Hanover Street

Building society Woolwich	227
Fashion FM **R.M. Williams**	223

Maddox Street

Jewellers **Pravins**	221
Telecom **Electronics**	219
British cloth **Tops**	217
Hairdressing salon **Alan d**	215
Cyprus Government Tourist Office	213
Fashion FM, childrenswear **Scottish Wear**	207-9
Moroccan National Tourist Office	205
Shoes FM **Clark's**	203

Great Marlborough Street

214-222	**LIBERTY** STORE
212	Barclays Bank
208	**The Gap** Fashion FM

Conduit Street

Shoes FM **Church's**	201
The Pen Shop	199
Fashion FM **Racing Green**	193-7
Fashion FM **The Scotch House**	189
Jewellers **Peter Trevor**	189
Textiles **Court**	187
Israeli airline El Al	185

Foubert's Place

204	**Jaeger** Fashion FM
198	**House of Chinacraft** China & glass
188	**Hamleys** Toys
178	**Warner Bros Studio Store** Gifts
176	**Levis Store** Fashion FM
172	**Episode** Fashion F
170	**Mappin & Webb** Jewellers
160	**Next** Fashion FM
158	**Waterford/Wedgwood** China & glass
156	**British Airways Travellers Shop**

New Burlington Place

Shoes FM **Viyella**	181-183
Royal Jordanian airline Alia	177
Cashmeres **House of Cashmere**	175
Bureau de change	173
Saudi Arabian Airlines	171
Fashion FM **Regents**	169

Regent Street continued

Left	No.	No.	Right
New Burlington Street			**Beak Street**
Fashion M **Bellini**	167	154	**Lawleys** English china & glass
Fashion FM **Burberrys**	157	152	**Bally** Shoes FM
Gifts **Past Times**	155	144	**Gap Kids** Childrenswear
The English Teddy Bear Company	153	140	**The Disney Store** Gifts
		138	**The Cashmere Gallery** Cashmeres
New Burlington Mews		134	**Reject China Shop** China
		132	Lloyds Bank
Fashion M **Cougar**	151		
Fabrics **The Woollens Centre**	149		
Heddon Street			
Singapore Airlines	143-147		
Fashion FM **Oxfords**	143		
Knitwear & fashions FM **The Scottish Cashmere Co**	141		
China **Rosenthal**	139		
Jewellers **Thomas**	137		
Midland Bank	133		
Heddon Street			**Regent Place**
Fashion FM **The Highlands**	129	130	**Boodle & Dunthorpe** Jewellers
Fashion FM **Cyril**	129	124	**Watches of Switzerland**
Fashion M **Hunters**	125	122	**Tie Rack** Fashion FM
Fashion M **Sacci**	121a	120	**Evans** Fashion F
Fabrics **Fine Textiles**	121	114	**Burton/Dorothy Perkins** Fashion FM
Pens **Pencraft**	119	112	**Garrard** Gold & silversmiths
Bureau de change A.M.B.	117		
TSB Bank	115		
Vigo Street			**Glasshouse Street**
Fashion M **Austin Reed**	103	100	**Aquascutum** Fashion FM
Shoes FM **K Shoes**	101	90	**Dunn & Co** Fashion M
The London Textile Co	99	88	**Moss Bros** Fashion M
Restaurant **The Veeraswamy**	99	86	**The Scotch House** Fashion FM
		82	**MGM** Cinema
Swallow Street			**Quadrant Arcade**
Ties, shirts M **Off The Cuff**	93	80	**Astuces** Fashion F
Meditation centre **Inner Space**	89	76	**Alexandra** Workwear
Handbags & luggage **Salisbury**	87	74a	**Angus Steak House** Restaurant
Bureau de change & ticket agency Eurochange	83		
China & glass **Chinacraft**	71		**Air Street**
Opticians **Paris-Miki**	69		
		70	**Café Royal** Restaurant & bars
		64	**Paul & Shark** Fashion M
Air Street		62	**House of Cashmeres** Cashmeres
		60	**Pringle** Fashion FM
Sock Shop	61	52	Barclays Bank
Fashion M **Lacoste**	59		
Fashion F **Jigsaw**	57		
Fashion FM **Tie Rack**	55		
Records, CDs & cassettes **Tower Records**	49		

Piccadilly Circus

King's Road

Left	No.	No.	Right
Sloane Square			**Sloane Square**
STORE **PETER JONES**			Sloane Square
		1	**Bliss** Chemist
		1	**Health Shop**
		1	Barclays Bank
		3	**Knickerbox** Lingerie
		5	**Whistles** Fashion F
		7	**Kookai** Fashion F
		9	Post Office
		11	**The Coffee Shop**
		11	**HoHo** Chinese restaurant
		13	**Naf Naf** Fashion FM
		15	**Osh Kosh B'gosh** Childrenswear
		21	Ladbrokes Bookmakers
		23	**Forbuoys** Newsagents & tobacconists
		25	**Lazer** Fashion M
		27	Eurochange Bureau de change
		29	**Gianni Ricci** Fashion M
		31	**Astuces** Fashion F
			Duke of York's Headquarters
Cadogan Gardens			
Childrenswear & accessories **Trotters**	34		
Children's playthings **Early Learning Centre**	36		
Fashion F **Hampstead Bazaar**	38		
Sportswear **King's Road Sporting Club**	40-42		
Fashion M **Cecil Gee**	44		
Wine Bar **Blushes**	52		
Natural beauty products **The Body Shop**	54		
Fashion FM **Jeans West**	54		
Restaurant **Pizza Hut**	56		
Chemist **Boots**	58		
Shoes FM **Russell & Bromley**	64		
Sock Shop	68		
Blacklands Terrace			
Fashion FM, childrenswear, home furnishings **Next**	72		

King's Road continued

Lincoln Street

Boulangerie/pâtisserie **Guys & Dolls**	74
Fashion F **Oasis**	76
Take-away food **Prêt à Manger**	80
Fashion FM **Esprit**	82
Shoes FM **Hobbs**	84
Fashion F **Boules**	86
Fashion FM **Stefanel**	88
Shoes FM **Cable & Co**	90
Shoes FM **Bally**	92
Fashion F **Benetton**	94
Fashion F **Warehouse**	96
Restaurant **The Chelsea Kitchen**	98
Shoes FM **Office London**	100
Gifts **Past Times**	102
Gifts **Notting Hill Housing Trust**	104
Fashion F **House of Carligry**	106
Fashion FM **Tie Rack**	108

Anderson Street

Building Society Chelsea	112
Fashion M **Reiss**	114

Tryon Street

Fashion FM **The Leather Warehouse**	118
Shoes FM **Bertie**	118
Fashion F **The Vestry**	120
Fashion FM & childrenswear **Gap**	122
SHOPPING MALL KINGS WALK	
Fashion F **Kookai**	124
Fashion M **Woodhouse**	124a
Shoes FM **Shellys**	124b
Fashion F **Jigsaw**	124c
Fashion M **Jigsaw**	126
Shoes FM **Ravel**	128
Bureau de change Chequepoint	130
Lingerie **Eda**	132

Bywater Street

Beauty products & comestibles **Crabtree & Evelyn**	134
Fashion F **Harvest**	136
Building society Abbey National	138

Markham Square

Fashion FM **French Connection**	140
Greetings cards **Scribbler**	146

Markham Street

Chemist **Boots**	150
Restaurant **Toad Hall**	152
Stationery **Ryman**	152
Books **Dillons**	152

Jubilee Place

Lloyds Bank	164
Fashion FM **Chelsea Leather**	168
Film processing **Snappy Snaps**	170
Restaurant **Choy's**	172
Shoes FM **Blue Velvet**	174
Opticians **Chelsea Eye Centre**	176

Burnsall Street

London Car Telephones	178
Fashion F **Work Shop**	178a
Confectioner **Thorntons**	182
Hairdresser **Terence Renati**	182a
Teas & coffees **Whittard**	184
Fashion FM **Soldier Blue**	184a

Cheltenham Terrace

33	National Westminster Bank
33a	**Blazer** *Fashion M*
33b	**Dune** *Shoes FM*
33c	**Accessorize** *Accessories*
33d	**Monsoon** *Fashion F*
33e	**Karen Millen** *Fashion F*
33f	**David Clulow** *Opticians*
33g	**Pied à Terre** *Shoes FM*
33h	**Our Price** *Records, CDs & cassettes*

Walpole Street

35	**Safeway** *Supermarket*

Royal Avenue

49	**McDonald's** *Restaurant*
51	**Miso** *Designer clearance store*
53	**Joseph** *Designer clearance store*
55	**Oddbins** *Wine merchants*
57	**Jones** *Shoes FM*
59	**Karen Millen** *Fashion F*

Wellington Street

61	**Dentics** *Dentist*
63	**Renegade** *Shoes FM*
65	**Sonico Jeans** *Fashion FM*
67	**Babe Power** *Fashion F*
67a	**Sacha** *Shoes FM*
69	**End** *Fashion F*

Smith Street

69a	**Sissors** *Hairdressing salon*
71	**Morgan** *Fashion F*
73	**Bruce Jeremy** *Fashion F*
75	**New Man** *Fashion M*
77	**Benihana** *Restaurant*
83	**Z.K. Bennet** *Shoes F*
85	**MARKS & SPENCER** *STORE*
95	**The Pier** *Household goods & furnishings*
99	**Woodhouse** *Fashion M*
	Car Park
105	**Anokhi & Jaipur** *Household goods*
107	**Stocks** *Nightclub*
109a	**R. Soles** *Leather boots*
109	**M.A.C.** *Cosmetics*
113	**Leather Classics** *Leatherwear FM*
115	**Kodo** *Fashion F*

Radnor Walk

119	**Chelsea Potter** *Pub*
121	**The Common Market** *Fashion FM*
123	**Lush** *Natural cosmetics*
123a	**Awards** *Fashion FM*

Shawfield Street

125	**Wax Lyrical** *Candles*
127	**Picasso** *Restaurant*
129	**Koko** *Fashion F*
137	**Basia Zarsycka** *Bridalwear, shoes, jewellery*
139	**Quincy** *Fashion M*
141	**Edwina Ronay** *Fashion F*

King's Road continued

Flood Street

Dry cleaners **Sketchley**	186	145	**Jaeger** Fashion FM
Fashion F **Snoops**	186a	147	**Paramount Original Studio Clothing** Fashion FM
Accessories F **Janet Fitch**	188	149	**Omcar** Shoes FM
Fashion F **Apple Tree**	190	151	**Shoe Repairs & Things** Shoe repair
Natural goods **Natural Fact**	192	153	**Boy** Fashion M
Candles **Angelic**	196	155	**Original Levi's Store** Fashion FM
Supermarket **Waitrose**	198	155a	Chelsea Methodist Church
Chelsea Cinema	206	157	**Hittite** Fashion F
Pub **The Trafalgar**	200	159	**Skindeep** Leather fashion FM
Furnishings **Habitat**	206	161	**The Boot Store** Shoes M
		163	**Docklands** Shoes FM

Chelsea Manor Street

Chelsea Manor Street

National Westminster Bank	224		TOWN HALL
Post Office	232		Citizen's Advice Bureau
Furnishings **Heal's**	234	181	**Chenil Galleries** Antiques
		183	**The Garage** Designer fashion FM
		185	**David Clulow** Opticians
Sydney Street		187	**Photo-Optix** Cameras
		191	**Phlip** Fashion FM
		193	**Steinberg & Tolkien** Antique clothing & jewellery
COUNCIL OFFICES	250	195	**Henry J Bean's Bar & Grill** Bar
		199	**Prime Video** Videos
		203	**Chelsea Audio-Visual Centre**
Dovehouse Street		205	**Pucci Pizza** Italian restaurant
		207	**Givans** Linen
CHELSEA FIRE STATION		209	**Oddbins** Wine merchants

Manresa Road

Oakley Street

KING'S COLLEGE LONDON

Glebe Place

		219	**David Pettifer** Antiques
		221	**My Old Dutch** Restaurant
		237	**Chelsea Food Fayre**
		239	**Z.K. Bennet** Fashion F

Bramerton Street

Carlyle Square

		241	**Designers Sale Studio** Fashion F
		243	**The Holding Company** Storage boxes
		243a	**Joanna Booth** Antiques
		245	**Made in Italy** Restaurant
		245a	**Chelsea Antique Market**
		247	**Joanna Booth** Antiques
		249	**Made In Italy** Restaurant
		251	**S. Borris** Delicatessen
		253	**Chelsea Antique Market**
		255	**Isaac. T. Lloyd** Chemist
		257	**Newsagents**
		259	**Green & Stone** Artists' materials
		263	**Ellessential** Hairdressing salon
		265	**Holme Place** Launderers & drycleaners
		271	**Designers Guild** Furnishings
		271b	**The Stockpot** Restaurant
Estate agents De Groot Collis	296	275	**David Tron** Antiques
Pub **Cadogan Arms**	298	277	**Designers Guild** Fabric & wallpapers

Old Church Street

Old Church Street

		279	MGM Cinema
Interior designers **Osborne & Little**	304	279	**Mr Light** Lighting
Antiques **Godson & Coles**	310	279	**Europa Foods** Supermarket
Restaurant **Le Gourmet**	312	279c	**Delcor** Interiors
Artists' materials **Chelsea Art Stores**	314	281	**Brats** Gifts & cards
Restaurant **Bar Central**	316	283	**Wilde One's** Ethnic fashion & gifts
Maps & prints **Old Church Galleries**	320	285	**Shoefax** Shoes FM
Furniture **Shaker**	322	287	**Raffles** Club
Furniture **Sofa Workshop**	324	289	**Designer Sample Store** Fashion F
Carpets **Bernadout**	328	289a	**Buona Sera** Restaurant
Restaurant **Lo Spuntino**	330	289	**Joanna's Tent** Fashion FM & childrenswear
Restaurant **Big Easy**	334		
Furniture **William Yeoward**	336		
Restaurant **Rotisserie Jules**	338		**Paultons Square**
Antiques **Acar**	340		
Restaurant **Thierry's**	342		
Fashion F **Brora**	344	307	**Chrysalis** Persian & Eastern rugs
Barclays Bank	348	309	**Million Dollar Sports** Sportswear
		311	**Chelsea Rare Books** Bookshop
		313	**Kaffee Opera** Coffee shop
The Vale		317	**Gregor Schumi** Hairdressing salon
		319	**J. & F. E. Simpson** Jewellers
		321	**Rococo** Chocolates
Fashion M **The Bad Apple**	350		
Fashion M **Nigel Hall**	350		
Designer fashion FM **The Bluebird Garage**	350		
Kings Food & Wines	350b		
Fashion M **Daniel James**	352		**Beaufort Street**
National Westminster Bank	352a		

Entertainment & Nightlife

From dance music to jazz, casino to comedy, London has it all – if you know where to look. And if you're starving in the small hours a number of restaurants are only too happy to oblige. London's nightlife can be expensive, but it needn't break the bank – why not catch a nightbus or join the real night owls in one of the all-night cafés, then catch the first tube home to bed! For more detailed information see *Nicholson's London Nightlife Guide*.

Artsline: *0171-388 2227 offers free advice and information on access to arts and entertainment for disabled people.*
Restaurant Services: *0181-888 8080 offers free advice and reservations. Mon-Fri 09.00-20.00.*
Theatreline
Information about West End productions and ticket availability. Dial (0891) 559 followed by 900 (for musicals), 901 (plays), 902 (comedies) or 903 (thrillers).

THEATRE TICKET AGENCIES

Fenchurch Booking Agency   96 D1
94 Southwark St SE1. 0171-928 8585. A.V.
First Call
0171-240 1000. A.Ax.Dc.V.
Keith Prowse
0171-420 0000. A.Ax.Dc.V.
Society of London Theatre   82 D6
Half-Price Ticket Booth (SOLT)
Leicester Sq WC2. Unsold tickets at half price on the day of the performance from the pavilion on the south side of Leicester Square.

Open from 12.00 (for matinées) & 14.30-18.30 (for evening performances). Maximum 4 tickets. No credit cards.
Ticketmaster UK Ltd   85 F6
0171-344 4444. A.Ax.V.

ARTS CENTRES

Barbican Centre   85 E1
Silk St EC2. 0171-638 8891. Several arts venues in one – a concert hall, two theatres, three cinemas, a public library, an art gallery and sculpture court. Box office *open Mon-Sun 09.00-20.00.*
Institute of Contemporary Arts   94 D2
The Mall SW1. 0171-930 3647. A good range of arts entertainment under one roof. Three galleries, a theatre, two cinemas, video reference library, arts bookshop, bar and restaurant. Membership required, day membership available (usually included in the ticket price). *Open Mon-Sun 12.00-01.00* (galleries to *19.30, to 21.30 Fri*).
South Bank Centre   95 H1
South Bank SE1. Recorded information: 0171-633 0932. One of the best- known arts complexes in Britain with plenty of choice from film and theatre to music and dance. It houses the National Theatre, the Royal Festival Hall, RFH2 – Queen Elizabeth Hall, RFH3 – Purcell Room (see pages 52-55 for details and telephone numbers), plus the Hayward Gallery (see page 22), the National Film Theatre (0171-928 3232) and the Museum of the Moving Image (see page 19). Restaurants, cafés and bars. A.Ax.Dc.V.

South Bank Centre

LIVE ENTERTAINMENT

CLASSICAL MUSIC, OPERA, BALLET, AND DANCE

Barbican Hall   **85 E1**
Barbican Centre, Silk St EC2. 0171-638 8891.
Home of the London Symphony Orchestra,
which offers three one-month-long seasons
during the year. Excellent acoustics. Venue
for opera, jazz, and light classical music. Box
office *open 09.00-20.00 Mon-Sun*. A.Ax.V.

London Coliseum   **83 E6**
St Martin's Lane WC2. 0171-632 8300. Built
in 1904, with a splendidly ornate interior,
London's largest theatre seats 2400. Home of
the English National Opera and host to visiting
dance and ballet companies every summer.
Stand-by tickets for all productions are sold at
reduced prices on the day of the performance.
Box office *open 10.00-20.00 Mon-Sat*. A.Ax.Dc.V.

The Place   **72 D4**
17 Duke's Rd WC1. 0171-387 0031. Innovative
and modern dance venue. It is home to the
Richard Alston Dance Company, Random
Dance Company and others. Box office *open
10.00-18.00 Mon-Fri, 12.00-18.00 Sat (to 20.00 if
a performance)*. A.V.

Royal Albert Hall   **91 F4**
Kensington Gore SW7. 0171-589 8212. Recorded
information: (0898) 500252. The first-ever
gramophone concert was held here in 1906.
Now used for rock, folk and jazz, but mainly
for classical concerts. Famous for the annual
Promenade concerts *Jul-Sep* (see page 15).
New home of the Royal Philharmonic
Orchestra. Box office *open 09.00-21.00 Mon-
Sun*. A.Ax.V.

London Coliseum

Royal Festival Hall   **95 H2**
South Bank Centre SE1. 0171-928 8800/960
4242. Built in 1951 for the Festival of Britain,
the Royal Festival Hall is one of the more
prominent buildings in the South Bank Arts
complex. With a 3000-seat capacity, it hosts
choral and orchestral concerts. Box office
open 10.00-21.00 Mon-Sun. A.Ax.Dc.V.

RFH2 (Queen Elizabeth Hall)   **95 H1**
South Bank Centre SE1. 0171-928 8800/960
4242. Seats 1100, and usually stages chamber
music, orchestral concerts and solo recitals.
Also film shows. Box office *open 10.00-21.00
Mon-Sun*. A.Ax.Dc.V.

RFH3 (Purcell Room)   **95 H1**
South Bank Centre SE1. 0171-928 8800/960
4242. Popular for its intimacy. Hosts mainly
chamber music and solo concerts. Box office
open 10.00-21.00 Mon-Sun. A.Ax.Dc.V.

Royal Opera House   **83 F4**
Covent Garden WC2. 0171-304 4000. Recorded
information: 0171-836 6903. The home of the
Royal Ballet and the English National Opera
is the most lavish theatre in London and the
greatest stage for British opera and ballet.
Sixty-five tickets are reserved for sale at the
box office in Floral St from *10.00* on the day of
the performance only (except for gala performances). If the performance is a sell-out,
standing-room tickets are made available in
the foyer. Be warned – queues have been
known to start at dawn! Box office *open 10.00-
20.00 Mon-Sat*. A.Ax.Dc.V. *To close for re-
development in 1997*.

Sadler's Wells   **74 A5**
Rosebery Ave EC1. 0171-713 6000. The first
theatre here was a "musick" house built in
1683 by Thomas Sadler as a side attraction to
his medicinal well. Now stages productions
by leading British and foreign companies,
and is the most popular dance theatre in
London. Box office *open 10.00-20.00 Mon-Sat*.
A.Ax.Dc.V.

St John Smith Square   **95 E6**
Smith Sq SW1. 0171-222 1061. A unique 18thC
church whose appearance has been likened
to an upturned footstool. Regular lunchtime
and evening concerts featuring solo recitals,
chamber music, orchestral and choral works.
Restaurant, art exhibitions in the crypt. Box
office *open 10.00-17.00 Mon-Fri (to 18.00 on
night of a performance)*. A.V.

Wigmore Hall   **81 E4**
36 Wigmore St W1. 0171-935 2141. Well-loved
by artists and audiences alike for its wonderful
acoustics and intimate atmosphere. Stages all
kinds of classical music. *Sun morning* coffee
concerts. Tickets usually cheap, but those for
popular concerts go very quickly. Box office

open 10.00-20.30 Mon-Sat (telephone bookings until 19.00). A.Ax.Dc.V.

JAZZ, FOLK AND ROCK

Academy
211 Stockwell Rd, Brixton SW9. 0171-924 9999. Atmospheric rock venue. The bars are well-staffed, and the sloping floor means you can see the band, even if you're marooned at the back. Also hosts dance, opera and theatre. *Open to 23.00* on night of performance. Box office *open 10.00-19.00 Mon-Fri, 11.00-18.00 Sat.* A.Dc.V.

Astoria   82 D3
157 Charing Cross Rd WC2. 0171-434 0403. A semi-converted theatre with 600 seats upstairs, four bars and a huge dancefloor. Also a club venue. Box office *open 10.00-18.00 Mon-Sat.* No credit cards.

The Blue Note   75 G6
1 Hoxton Square N1. 0171-729 8440. East London's new jazz venue in the former home of The Bass Clef. *Closing times vary – phone for details.* A.Ax.Dc.V.

The Forum
9-17 Highgate Rd, Kentish Town NW5. 0171-284 1001. Formerly the Town & Country Club, this remains one of the best live music venues in London. Rock, folk and jazz. *Open to 23.00, to 02.00 Fri & Sat.* A.Ax.Dc.V.

Marquee

Hammersmith Apollo
Queen Caroline St, Hammersmith W6. 0181-741 4868. Formerly the Hammersmith Odeon, this is west London's legendary live music venue. Plays host to a wide range of musical talents. Box office *open 10.00-18.00 Mon-Sat.* A.Ax.V.

100 Club   80 D4
100 Oxford St W1. 0171-636 0933. Friendly and comfortable basement club, historically the home of British traditional jazz. One of the best places in London for 'trad', but also caters well for fans of modern jazz, blues, swing and rockabilly. *Opening times vary – phone for details.* No credit cards.

Marquee   82 D4
105 Charing Cross Rd WC2. 0171-437 6603. One of the original rock clubs. In the 1960s any rocker worth his salt played here. Nowadays the Marquee and its bands tend to be less prestigious, but it's still a popular, lively spot. *Open to 03.00 Thur, to 04.00 Fri, to 06.00 Sat.* Box office *open 07.00-14.00 Thur, 11.00-15.00 Fri & Sat – liable to change.* A.V.

Rock Garden   83 F5
6-7 Covent Garden Piazza WC2. 0171-240 3961. Beneath the restaurant of the same name, a selection of starry-eyed young bands play in a converted banana warehouse. You might hear tomorrow's stars – U2 and Dire Straits once played here. *Open to 03.00, to 06.00 Fri & Sat.* A.V.

Ronnie Scott's   82 C4
47 Frith St W1. 0171-439 0747. One of Europe's foremost jazz centres, and reputedly the best in London, attracting a succession of big-name jazz men and women. The atmosphere can be typically dark and smoky on a busy night. *Open to 03.00 Mon-Sat.* A.Ax.Dc.V.

Wembley Arena
Empire Way, Wembley, Middx. 0181-900 1234. Huge indoor venue for major concerts with big-name bands and spectacular lightshows. Box Office *open 09.00-21.00.* A.Ax.Dc.V.

COMEDY

Comedy Store   82 D5
1 Oxenden St WC2. (0426) 914433. *The* London comedy venue where a lively array of comedians line up for a 2-3 hour show. The audience is encouraged to join in. *2-hr shows at 20.00 & 24.00 Tue-Sun.* Improvisation from the famous Comedy Store Players *Wed & Sun 20.00.*

Jongleurs
The Cornet, 49 Lavender Gdns SW11. 0171-924 2766. Also Jongleurs Camden Lock, 211-

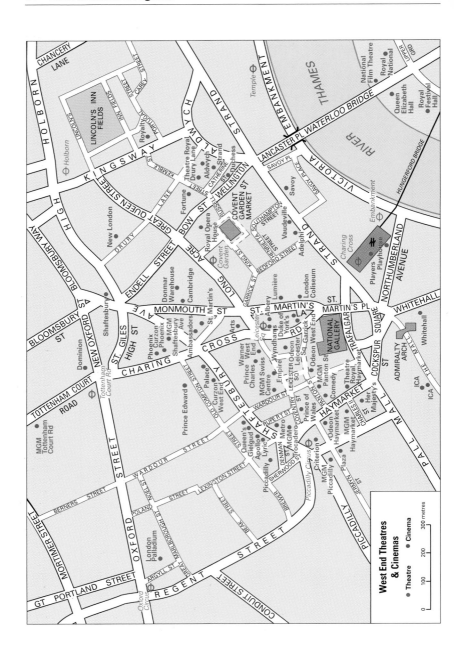

West End Theatres
& Cinemas

● Theatre   ● Cinema

216 Chalk Farm Rd NW1. Very popular venue offering comedy, visual acts, music and dance. Show package offers buffet, two comedians, two speciality acts and disco. Essential to book. *Fri 21.00, Sat 19.00 & 23.00; followed by a disco.*

THEATRES (WEST END)

Adelphi   **83 F6**
Strand WC2. 0171-344 0055. Musicals including *Me and My Girl.*

Albery   **83 E5**
St Martin's Lane WC2. 0171-369 1730. Originally the New Theatre. Renamed in 1973. Musicals, comedy and drama.

Aldwych   **83 G4**
Aldwych WC2. 0171-836 6404. Former London home of the Royal Shakespeare Company. Plays, comedies and musicals.

Ambassadors   **82 D4**
West St WC2. 0171-836 6111. Small theatre, the original home of *The Mousetrap* until it moved to nearby St Martin's.

Apollo   **82 C5**
Shaftesbury Ave W1. 0171-416 6070. Old tradition of musical comedy. Now presents musicals, comedy and drama.

Apollo Victoria   **94 A6**
17 Wilton Rd SW1. 0171-630 6262. This auditorium was completely transformed to accommodate the hit rollerskating railway musical *Starlight Express.*

Comedy   **82 C6**
Panton St SW1. 0171-369 1731. Good intimate theatre showing unusual comedy and small-cast plays.

Criterion   **82 C6**
Piccadilly Circus W1. 0171-369 1747. Listed building which has been renovated in recent years. Houses the only underground auditorium in London.

Drury Lane (Theatre Royal)   **83 G5**
Catherine St WC2. 0171-494 5062. Operated under Royal Charter by Thomas Killigrew in 1663, it has been burnt or pulled down and rebuilt four times. Nell Gwynne performed here and Orange Moll sold her oranges. Garrick, Mrs Siddons, Kean and others played here. General policy now is vast musical productions like *Miss Saigon.*

Duchess   **83 G5**
Catherine St WC2. 0171-494 5075. Opened 1929. Plays, serious drama, light comedy and musicals.

Duke of York's   **83 E6**
St Martin's Lane WC2. 0171-836 5122. Built by 'Mad (Violet) Melnotte' in 1892. Associated with names like Frohman, George Bernard Shaw, Granville Barker, Chaplin and the

Ballet Rambert. *Royal Court productions will be staged here during renovations.*

Fortune   **83 F4**
Russell St WC2. 0171-836 2238. Small compared with its neighbour, Drury Lane. Intimate revues (Peter Cook and Dudley Moore shot to fame here in *Beyond the Fringe*), musicals and modern drama.

Garrick   **83 E6**
Charing Cross Rd WC2. 0171-494 5085. Built 1897. Notable managers included Bouchier and Jack Buchanan. Varied bills.

Gielgud   **82 C5**
Shaftesbury Ave W1. 0171-494 5065. Formerly the Globe, renamed in honour of Sir John Gielgud. A wide variety of successful plays and comedies.

Haymarket (Theatre Royal)   **82 D6**
Haymarket SW1. 0171-930 8800. Built in 1721 as the 'Little Theatre in the Hay', it became Royal 50 years later. The present theatre was built by Nash in 1821 and is enlivened by the ghost of Mr Buckstone, Queen Victoria's favourite actor-manager. He no doubt approves of the policy to present plays of quality.

Her Majesty's   **94 C1**
Haymarket SW1. 0171-494 5400. Fine Victorian baroque theatre founded by Beerbohm Tree. Successes include *West Side Story, Fiddler on the Roof, Amadeus* and, most recently, Lloyd Webber's *Phantom of the Opera.*

London Palladium   **82 A4**
8 Argyll St W1. 0171-494 5020. Second in size to the Coliseum, it houses top variety shows.

Lyric   **82 C5**
Shaftesbury Ave W1. 0171-494 5045. Oldest theatre in Shaftesbury Avenue (built 1888). Eleonora Duse, Sarah Bernhardt, Owen Nares and Tallulah Bankhead all had long runs here.

Lyric Hammersmith
King St W6. 0181-741 2311. Rebuilt and restored to original Victorian splendour inside a modern shell. Spacious foyers, bar, restaurant and terrace. Wide-ranging productions.

Mermaid   **84 D5**
Puddle Dock, Blackfriars EC4. 0171-236 2221. Plays and musicals. Restaurant and two bars overlooking the Thames.

National   **95 H1**
South Bank SE1. 0171-928 2252. Complex of three theatres, the Olivier, Lyttelton and Cottesloe. Home of the Royal National Theatre Company. Stages a wide mixture of plays in repertory, including new works, revivals, Shakespeare and musicals. Restaurant, bars.

New London   **83 F3**
Drury Lane WC2. 0171-405 0072. Can convert from a 900-seat conventional theatre to an intimate theatre-in-the-round within minutes. Opened 1972 on the site of the old Winter

Gardens. The hit musical *Cats* is well-established here.

Old Vic   **96 B3**
Waterloo Rd SE1. 0171-928 7616. Built 1818. For a long time the home of the National Theatre Company, then housed the Prospect Theatre Company. It now shows plays and musicals amid recreated Victorian decor.

Palace   **82 D4**
Shaftesbury Ave W1. 0171-434 0909. Listed building. Originally intended by Richard D'Oyly Carte to be the Royal English Opera House, but eventually became the Palace Theatre of Varieties. Staged performances by Pavlova and Nijinski. Now owned by Sir Andrew Lloyd Webber whose musical *Jesus Christ Superstar* enjoyed a record run here; *Les Misérables* is its latest success story.

Phoenix   **82 D4**
Charing Cross Rd WC2. 0171-369 1733. A large theatre. Comedies, plays and musicals.

Piccadilly   **82 C5**
Denman St W1. 0171-369 1734. A pre-war theatre which showed the first season of 'Talkies' in Britain. Varied post-war history of light comedy, plays and musicals. Royal Shakespeare Company productions staged here. Transformed into a cabaret theatre 1983.

Playhouse   **95 E1**
Northumberland Ave WC2. 0171-839 4401. Edwardian theatre used as a BBC studio and then closed in 1975. Restored to former glory and re-opened in 1987. Stages musicals, serious drama and comedies.

Prince Edward   **82 D4**
Old Compton St W1. 0171-734 8951. Started life as the 'London Casino' in 1936 and has also been a cinema. Now a large theatre staging musicals. The hit show *Evita* ran for 2900 performances here.

Prince of Wales   **82 C6**
Coventry St W1. 0171-839 5989. Rebuilt 1937, this large, modern theatre has housed many musicals.

Queen's   **82 C5**
Shaftesbury Ave W1. 0171-494 5040. Very successful between the wars. Still presents good drama and varied productions.

Royal Court   **103 E2**
Sloane Sq SW1. 0171-730 1745. Home of the English Stage Company, which produces many major experimental plays. *Productions will transfer to Duke of York's during renovations starting late 1996.*

St Martin's   **83 E5**
West St WC2. 0171-836 1443. Intimate playhouse with unusual polished teak doors. *The Mousetrap* continues its record run here having transferred from the Ambassadors.

Savoy   **83 G6**
Strand WC2. 0171-836 8888. Entrance is in the forecourt of the Savoy Hotel. Produces a variety of plays, comedies and musicals. Has been restored to its Art Deco splendour after the interior was destroyed by fire in 1990.

Shaftesbury   **82 C5**
Shaftesbury Ave WC2. 0171-379 5399. Home of the Theatre of Comedy Company.

Strand   **83 G5**
Aldwych WC2. 0171-930 8800. Presents a mixture of straight plays, comedies and musicals.

Vaudeville   **83 F6**
Strand WC2. 0171-836 9987. Listed building which originally ran farce and burlesque (hence the name), then became straight, which for the most part it remains.

Victoria Palace   **94 A6**
Victoria St SW1. 0171-834 1317. Musicals, variety shows and plays. Once home of the *Crazy Gang* and the *Black and White Minstrel Show*, the musical *Buddy* is a recent success.

Whitehall   **95 E2**
14 Whitehall SW1. 0171-867 1119. Splendid Art Deco interior. Now one of the Wyndham Theatres group staging varied productions.

Wyndham's   **83 E5**
Charing Cross Rd WC2. 0171-369 1736. Small, pretty and successful theatre founded by Sir Charles Wyndham, the famous actor-manager. Plays, comedy and musicals.

Young Vic   **96 B3**
66 The Cut SE1. 0171-928 6363. Young people's repertoire theatre mainly showing the classics and established modern plays, but also some new plays and musicals.

OPEN-AIR THEATRE

Holland Park Theatre   **89 H4**
Holland Park W8. 0171-602 7856. 700-seat open-air theatre staging dance, opera and theatre productions *Tue-Sat Jun-Aug. Check for times.* A.V.

Regent's Park Open Air Theatre   **71 E4**
Inner Circle, Regent's Park N1. 0171-486 2431. In a magical setting enclosed within the park. Plays by Shakespeare (*A Midsummer Night's Dream* is a perennial favourite) and others alternate from *end May-Sep*. Book in advance. Performances *20.00 Mon-Sat.* A.Ax.Dc.V.

NIGHTLIFE

NIGHTCLUBS

The following venues do not require membership and usually host one-night clubs; check for details in advance. Entry to most of the following clubs will be about **£5.00-£8.00** weekdays and **£10.00** at weekends.

Camden Palace
1a Camden High St, Camden NW1. 0171-387 0428. A huge, multi-storey former music hall. Spacious and lively, attracting a young trendy crowd. *Open to 02.30 Tue-Thur, to 04.30 Fri, to 03.30 Sat. Closed Sun.* No credit cards.

Electric Ballroom
184 Camden High St, Camden NW1. 0171-485 9006. This established no-frills venue has a capacity for 1100. Two clubs in one, offering anything from acid jazz to classic rock. Cafeteria serving snacks and breakfast. *Open to 02.00 Fri & Sat.* No credit cards.

Equinox   **82 D5**
Leicester Sq WC2. 0171-437 1446. Huge venue offering mainstream chart and dance music. Student nights *Tue & Wed. Open to 03.00 Mon-Thur, to 04.00 Fri & Sat.* A.Ax.V.

The Fridge
Town Hall Parade, Brixton Hill SW2. 0171-326 5100. Gay and lesbian club. Various one-nighters. No credit cards.

Hippodrome   **82 D5**
Cranbourn St WC2. 0171-437 4311. A black cave of brass and chrome illuminated by an amazing lighting system. Popular with young European tourists. Six bars, restaurant. *Open to 03.00 Mon-Thur, to 03.30 Fri & Sat. Closed Sun.* A.Ax.V.

Limelight   **82 D5**
136 Shaftesbury Ave W1. 0171-434 0572. Uniquely housed in a converted church, this club is a maze of wood-panelled passages and stairs leading to three levels. One-nighters range from rock to dance and reggae. *Open to 03.00 Mon-Sat. Closed Sun.* A.Ax.V.

Ministry of Sound   **96 D5**
103 Gaunt St SE1. 0171-378 6528. Huge New York-style venue offering the biggest sound system in Britain, big-name DJs, laser shows and a cinema. *Open to 07.00 Thur & Fri, to 10.00 Sat/Sun.* No credit cards.

Stringfellows   **83 E5**
16-19 Upper St Martin's Lane WC2. 0171-240 5534. Most celebrities have been photographed flashing their teeth and jewellery here. A la carte restaurant. *Open to 03.30. Closed Sun.* A.Ax.Dc.V.

Subterania   **77 G2**
12 Acklam Rd W10. 0181-960 4590. A trendy and friendly venue under the Westway flyover. Stylish interior with regular live music. Regular live bands. *Open to 01.30 Mon-Thur, to 02.30 Fri & Sat. Closed Sun.* A.V.

The Wag Club   **82 C5**
35-37 Wardour St W1. 0171-437 5534. Once the trendiest club in town, the Wag still

The Hippodrome

attracts an exuberant, young clientele. Weekend nights are very popular, and you may have difficulty gaining entry. *Open to 03.00 Tue-Thur, to 06.00 Fri & Sat. Closed Sun.* No credit cards.

DINNER AND ENTERTAINMENT

If you would rather sit and be entertained than dance the night away, make for one of the following venues. In most cases it is advisable to reserve in advance. Average cost of a three-course meal for one inclusive of VAT and service but without wine:

SS   - £10.00-£20.00
SSS   - £20.00-£30.00
SSS+ - £30.00 and over

Beefeater by the Tower of London   **98 D1**
Ivory House, St Katharine's Way E1. 0171-224 9000. A journey back to the age of the Tudors, over a five-course banquet. A juggler and a magician perform between courses, and Henry VIII appears in full costume to propose the toasts. *Advisable to reserve in advance. Open to 23.30. Closed Sun.* A.Ax.Dc.V. **SSS**+

The Cockney   **72 B6**
161 Tottenham Court Rd W1. 0171-224 9000. Traditional East End music hall entertainment, with Pearly Kings and Queens, buskers, and a honky-tonk piano. *Open to 23.30.* A.Ax.Dc.V. **SSS**+

Costa Dorada   **82 C3**
47-55 Hanway St W1. 0171-631 5117. Authentic Spanish establishment tucked away in a narrow street near Oxford Street. Flamenco dancers entertain while you dine on excellent

Spanish food. Lively atmosphere. *Open to 03.00 Mon-Sat.* A.Dc.V. **SSS**

Elysée 82 C2
13 Percy St W1. 0171-636 4804. There's a rumbustious atmosphere in this taverna-style restaurant, with traditional Greek dancing and entertainment. Roof garden open in the summer. *Open to 03.00 Mon-Sat.* Cabaret at *23.00, 01.00 & 02.30.* A.Ax.Dc.V. **SSS**

Flanagan's 80 D1
100 Baker St W1. 0171-935 0287. Phoney but fun Victorian dining rooms with sawdust on the floor, stalls and cockney sing-a-longs. Customers join in the singing between tucking into enormous plates of fish and chips. *Open to 22.30.* A.Ax.Dc.V. **SS**

Royal Garden Hotel, 90 D3
Royal Roof Restaurant
2-24 Kensington High St W8. 0171-937 8000. A Modern European restaurant with dinner dancing *Sat* evening. Excellent views over Kensington Gardens and Kensington Palace. *Open to 22.30, to 23.00 Sat.* A.Ax.Dc.V. **SSS+**

Southamptons 124 83 F1
and All That Jazz
124 Southampton Row WC1. 0171-405 1466. Great jazz accompanies the excellent and varied menu. *Open to 01.30 Mon-Sat, to 24.00 Sun.* A.Ax.V. **SS**

Talk of London 83 F3
Drury Lane, cnr Parker St WC2. 0171-224 9000. Modern theatre/restaurant featuring popular cabaret acts. Dancing to a resident band. French and international cuisine. *Open to 24.00.* A.Ax.Dc.V. **SSS+**

Terrazza Est 84 C4
109 Fleet St EC4. 0171-353 2680. Large basement restaurant known as the Spaghetti Opera for its superb, uplifting opera singing. Lively atmosphere. Set and a la carte menus. *Open to 23.00 Mon-Fri.* A.Ax.Dc.V. **SSS+**

Windows on the World 93 F2
Hilton Hotel, 22 Park Lane W1. 0171-493 8000. Diners are afforded intoxicating views over the city from 28 floors up. Excellent French cooking. Dance floor, live music. *Open to 02.00 Mon-Sat.* A.Ax.Dc.V. **SSS+**

CASINOS

You can enter a gaming house only as a member or a guest of a member. By law, when you join a gaming club you will not be admitted until you have filled in a declaration of your intent to gamble and 48 hours have elapsed from the time you signed this declaration. The number **(48)** after a club's name means this rule applies. **(M)** means that membership is necessary for entry.

Charlie Chester Casino (48) 82 C5
12 Archer St W1. 0171-734 0255. Nightclub

and casino. Smart American-style restaurant. **(M)** *Open to 04.00 Mon-Sun.* No credit cards.

Clermont Club (48) 81 H6
44 Berkeley Sq W1. 0171-493 5587. An 18thC town house, opulent and comfortable. Select and very expensive to join. Excellent à la carte restaurant with Arab cuisine. **(M)** *Open to 04.00 Mon-Sun.* A.Ax.Dc.V.

Golden Horseshoe (48) 78 D5
79-81 Queensway W2. 0171-221 8788. Casino with a bar and small restaurant. **(M)** *Open to 04.00 Mon-Sun.* A.Ax.Dc.V.

LATE-NIGHT EATING AND DRINKING

Bar Italia 82 C4
22 Frith St W1. 0171-437 4520. The most authentic Italian café in Soho. The decor and the atmosphere have changed little since the 1950s and it's always lively and vibrant. Unlicensed, but this doesn't detract from its popularity! *Open 24 hrs Mon-Sun.*

Bar Madrid 82 A3
4 Winsley St W1. 0171-436 4649. Large, lively and fairly authentic tapas bar. *Open to 03.00.* Closed Sun.

Bar Sol Ona 82 D4
17 Old Compton St W1. 0171-287 9932. Basement bar with lots of nooks and crannies in which to linger over your drinks, nibble tapas, and attempt to make yourself heard over the flamenco music. Attracts a friendly, party-minded clientele. *Open to 03.00, to 23.00 Sun.*

Harry's Bar 82 A5
19 Kingly St W1. 0171-434 0309. Do people go to Harry's because they have stayed out late, or do they stay out late because they're going to Harry's? After sampling the late-night cooked breakfast you'll realise this is a serious question. A nightclubbers' institution. *Open to 06.00.*

Lido 82 D5
41 Gerrard St W1. 0171-437 4437. Lots of people tell stories about how they found a wonderful Chinese restaurant that was still open at dawn. The chances are the restaurant in question was Lido, a busy and friendly establishment on two floors. *Open to 04.00.*

Los Locos 83 G4
24-26 Russell St WC2. 0171-379 0220. Good, cheap Tex-Mex food in a large authentic Mexican restaurant. Also at 14 Soho St W1. 0171-287 0005 (**82 C3**). Disco from *23.30* every night. *Open to 03.00.*

Up All Night 101 F5
325 Fulham Rd SW10. 0171-352 1996. As the name suggests: serves steaks, burgers, spaghetti *to 06.00.*

Travel, Information & Emergency Services

LONDON TRANSPORT

For the latest update on the travel situation call Travel Check (*24 hrs*) on 0171-222 1200.

London Transport Travel   **94 C5**
Information Centre
55 Broadway SW1. 0171-222 1234. For information about underground and bus services.

Docklands Light Railway information on 0171-918 4000.

Travelcards can be bought at any Underground station and give unlimited travel for one day, a week, a month or a year on the Underground, buses, Docklands Light Railway and Network SouthEast trains.

Underground trains operate between approx *05.30-00.15 Mon-Sat, 07.30-23.30 Sun.*

London buses run from approx *06.00-24.00 Mon-Sat, 07.30-23.30 Sun*. Nightbuses run from about *23.00-06.00*. All pass through Trafalgar Square (**94 D1**).

Docklands Light Railway (DLR) operates between *05.30-00.30 Mon-Fri, 06.00-00.30 Sat* and *07.30-23.30 Sun (Beckton branch does not run at weekends)*.

BRITISH RAIL STATIONS

Blackfriars   **84 C5**
Queen Victoria St EC4. 0171-928 5100.
Cannon Street   **85 G5**
Cannon St EC4. 0171-928 5100.
Charing Cross   **95 F1**
Strand WC2. 0171-928 5100.
Euston   **72 C4**
Euston Rd NW1. 0171-387 7070.
Fenchurch Street   **86 B5**
Fenchurch St EC3. 0171-928 5100.
King's Cross   **73 E2**
Euston Rd N1. 0171-278 2477.
Liverpool Street   **86 A2**
Liverpool St EC2. 0171-928 5100.
London Bridge   **97 H2**
Borough High St SE1. 0171-928 5100.
Marylebone   **70 C6**
Boston Place NW1. 0171-387 7070.
Moorgate   **85 G2**
Moorgate EC2. 0171-278 2477.

Paddington   **79 G3**
Praed St W2. 0171-262 6767.
St Pancras   **73 E2**
Euston Rd NW1. 0171-387 7070.
Victoria   **103 H1**
Terminus Place, Victoria St SW1.
0171-928 5100.
Waterloo/Waterloo International   **96 A3**
York Rd SE1. 0171-928 5100.

TAXIS

The famous London taxi cabs can be hailed in the street. A taxi is available for hire if the yellow 'taxi' sign above the windscreen is lit. All taxis have meters which the driver must use on all journeys within the Metropolitan Police District. Expect to pay extra for large amounts of luggage, journeys between *20.00-06.00, at weekends and Bank hols*. You can order a black cab by telephone *24 hrs* a day, but this will be more expensive than hailing one in the street as you will be charged for being picked up as well as taken to your destination.

Computer-cab 0171-286 0286.
Dial-a-Cab 0171-253 5000.
Radio Taxicabs 0171-272 0272.

MINICABS

These cannot be hailed in the street, and are indistinguishable from private cars. Unlike the black taxi cabs they are not licensed and neither the drivers nor their cars are subject to the same stringent tests, but they are cheaper on longer journeys. Negotiate the price with the company when you phone, or with the driver, *before* you start your journey. The following firms are open *24 hrs*.

Abbey Car Hire W2. 0171-727 2637.
Bartley Cars N5. 0171-226 7555.
Greater London Car Hire. 0181-340 2450.
Hyde Park Cars SW5. 0171-370 2020.

British Travel Centre   **82 A5**
12 Lower Regent St SW1. Personal callers only. *Open 09.00-18.30 Mon-Fri, 10.00-16.00 Sat & Sun (09.00-17.00 Sat in May-Sep only)*.

City of London Information Centre   **85 E4**
St Paul's Churchyard EC4. 0171-606 3030.
Open May-Sep 09.30-17.00 Mon-Sun; Oct-Apr 09.30-17.00 Mon-Fri, 09.30-12.30 Sat.

London Tourist Board   **103 H1**
Information Centre
Victoria Station Forecourt SW1. *Open Apr-Oct 08.00-19.00 Mon-Sun; Nov-Mar 08.00-19.00 Mon-Sat, to 16.00 Sun. 24-hr* recorded information service on (0839) 123456.

ACCOMMODATION

Accommodation Service of the   **103 H1**
London Tourist Board
London Tourist Board Information Centre, Victoria Station Forecourt SW1. (0839) 123435. *Open 08.00-19.00 Mon-Sun.* Charge.

Hotel Booking Service   **82 A5**
4 New Burlington Place W1. 0171-437 5052. *Open 09.30-17.30 Mon-Fri.* Free.

Hotel Reservations Centre   **103 G2**
10 Buckingham Palace Rd SW1. 0171-828 2425. *Open 09.00-18.00 Mon-Fri.* Free.

EMERGENCY SERVICES

CHEMISTS (LATE-NIGHT)

The local police station keeps a list of chemists and doctors available at all hours.

Bliss Chemist   **80 D4**
5 Marble Arch W1. 0171-723 6116. *Open 09.00-24.00 every day of the year.*

Boots   **82 C6**
Piccadilly Circus W1. 0171-734 6126. *Open 08.30-20.00 Mon-Fri, 09.00-20.00 Sat, 12.00-18.00 Sun.*

Warman Freed
45 Golders Green Rd, Golders Green NW11. 081-455 4351. *Open 08.30-24.00 every day of the year.*

CREDIT CARDS

If you have lost an **Access** or **Visa** card issued by a bank in the UK, contact the emergency number of the issuing bank:

Barclays
(01604) 230230. *24 hrs.*
Lloyds
(01702) 362988. *24 hrs.*
Midland
0181-450 3122. *24 hrs.*
National Westminster
(0113) 2778899. *24 hrs.*
Royal Bank of Scotland
(01702) 362988. *24 hrs.*

Contact the emergency numbers listed below if you have lost the following cards:

American Express
(01273) 696933. *24 hrs.*
Diners Club
(01252) 516261. *24 hrs.*
Eurocheque card
(0113) 2778899. *24 hrs.*

If you have lost a **Visa** or **Mastercard** issued abroad, contact the following:
Mastercard
(01702) 362988. *24 hrs.*
Visa
(01604) 230230. *24 hrs.*

HOSPITALS

Central London hospitals which operate *24-hr* casualty departments.

Chelsea & Westminster Hospital   **101 F5**
369 Fulham Rd SW10. 0181-746 8000.
Guy's Hospital   **97 H2**
St Thomas St SE1. 0171-955 5000.
Royal London Hospital   **87 G2**
(Whitechapel)
Whitechapel Rd E1. 0171-377 7000.
St Thomas' Hospital   **95 G5**
Lambeth Palace Rd SE1. 0171-928 9292.
University College Hospital   **72 B6**
Gower St WC1. 0171-387 9300.

LATE POST

Most post offices close at *17.30 Mon-Fri & 12.00 Sat.* However, there is one late-opening office in London:
Post Office   **94 D1**
24-28 William IV St, Trafalgar Sq WC2. 0171-930 9580. *Open 08.00-20.00 Mon-Sat.*

LOST PROPERTY

Airports
For property lost in the main airport buildings phone the British Airport Authority's Lost Property Office, Heathrow Airport, Middx. 0181-759 4321. Or contact the airport direct.

British Rail (trains)
If you lose something on a train, contact the station where the train you were on terminates. They will be able to inform you whether your belongings have been recovered, and if so, where they have been taken.

London Transport (Underground)   **70 D6**
Lost Property Office, 200 Baker St W1 (next to Baker St Station). For enquiries about lost property please call in person (or send another person with written authority) or apply by letter. No telephone enquiries. *Open 09.30-14.00 Mon-Fri. Closed Bank hols.*

Taxis
If you leave anything in a taxi, apply 15 Penton N1 (**74 A2**). 0171-833 0996.

POLICE STATIONS
The main police stations within a 3-mile radius of Piccadilly Circus.

City of London

Headquarters & all departments	**85 G4**
26 Old Jewry EC2. 0171-601 2222.	
Bishopsgate	**86 B2**
182 Bishopsgate EC2. 0171-601 2222.	
Snow Hill	**74 C3**
5 Snow Hill EC1. 0171-601 2222.	
Wood Street	**85 F3**
37 Wood Street EC2. 0171-601 2222.	

Metropolitan

Cannon Row	**95 F3**
Victoria Embankment SW1. 0171-925 1212.	
Charing Cross	**83 F6**
Agar Street WC2. 0171-240 1212.	
Chelsea	**92 B2**
2 Lucan Pl SW3. 0181-741 6212.	
Hyde Park	**92 B1**
North of Serpentine W2. 0171-706 8679.	
Islington	**74 B1**
2 Tolpuddle St N1. 0171-704 1212.	
Kensington	**90 A6**
72-74 Earl's Court Rd W8. 0181-741 6212.	
New Scotland Yard	**94 C5**
Broadway SW1. 0171-230 1212.	

Southwark	**97 E4**
323 Borough High St SE1. 0171-407 4759.	
West End Central	**82 A5**
27 Savile Row W1. 0171-494 1212.	

WHEELCLAMPING
If you are illegally parked or your vehicle is causing an obstruction, it may be wheelclamped or towed to a pound. In either case you will have to pay a substantial fine to recover your car.

If you get wheel-clamped, follow the instructions on the label attached to your vehicle. If the label is missing, phone 0171-747 4747 *(24 hours)* to find out which authority to contact. This line is operated by TRACE (Tow Away, Removal and Clamping Enquiries) who are located at 1st Floor, New Zealand House, 80 Haymarket SW1 (**94 D1**). Their offices are *open 08.00-20.00 Mon-Fri.*

If your car is missing, phone TRACE on the above number to find out if it has been removed to a pound and, if so, which one, how to get there by public transport and how to pay the fine.

TRACE publish visitors' guides (in English, French, German, Spanish, Italian and Dutch) giving advice on parking in London and how to avoid parking penalties. These are obtainable direct from TRACE, or from the London Tourist Board or Town Halls.

Tower Bridge

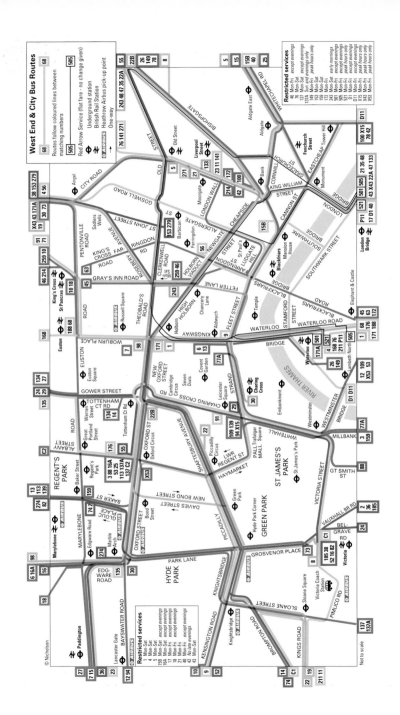

West End & City Bus Routes

NICHOLSON

MAPS

KEY TO MAP SYMBOLS

═════	Motorway/Dual Carriage	■ PO	Post Office
═════	Other Classified Road	𝑖	Tourist Information Centre
═════	Street Market	⚇ ODEON	Cinema
⇌ ⇌	British Rail Station	APOLLO	Theatre
⊖	London Underground Station	⊠ Hilton	Hotel
⊖	Docklands Light Railway Station	⌐ JAPAN	Embassy
⬭	Bus/Coach Station	▭ 8	Airline Office
P	Car Park	+	Church
WC	Public Toilet	☾	Mosque
■ POL	Police Station	✡	Synagogue

The reference grid on this atlas coincides with the Ordnance Survey National Grid System

▽A ▷3		Grid Reference
▲8		Page Continuation Number
25		OS National Grid Kilometre Square

Scale 1:10,000 (6.3 inches to 1 mile)

```
0          0.25          0.50          0.75 kilometre
|-----------|-------------|-------------|
0                        ¼                        ½ mile
```

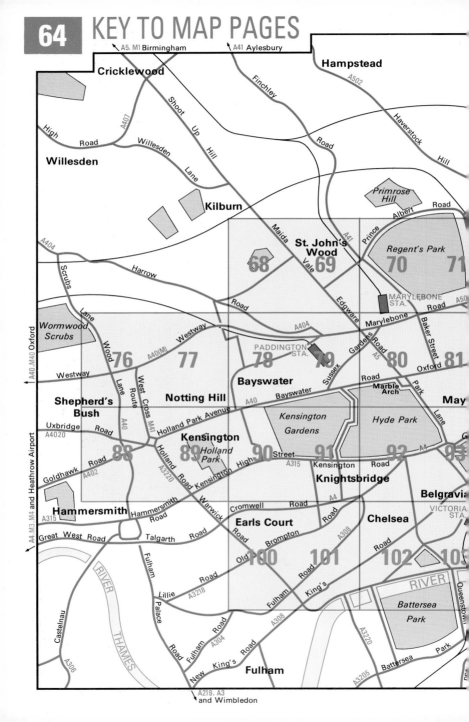

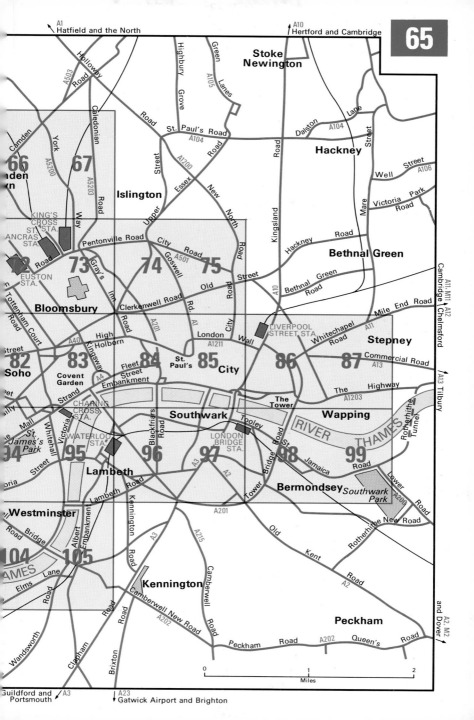

A1
Hatfield and the North

A10
Hertford and Cambridge

Stoke Newington

Hackney

Bethnal Green

Holloway Road
A503

Caledonian Road
A5203

Highbury Grove

Green Lanes
A105

St. Paul's Road
A104

Dalston Lane
A104

Mare Street

Well Street

Victoria Park Road
A106

66
**den
n**

Camden
York Way
A5200

67

Islington

Essex Road

Upper Street

New North Road
A1200

Kingsland Road

Hackney Road

A11,M11
Cambridge Chelmsford
A12

KING'S CROSS STA.
ST.PANCRAS STA.

EUSTON STA.

73

Pentonville Road

Gray's Inn Road

City Road
A501

Goswell Road

Old Street

74

75

Bethnal Green Road
A10

Mile End Road

Bloomsbury

Clerkenwell Road

High Holborn

Rd.
A1

City Road

London Wall
A1211

LIVERPOOL STREET STA.

Whitechapel Road

Stepney
A11

Tottenham Court Road
A40

Kingsway

Fleet Street

84
St. Paul's

85
City

86

87
Commercial Road
A13

82
Soho

83

Covent Garden

A4

Embankment
Strand

The Highway
A1203

The

CHARING CROSS STA.

Victoria

WATERLOO STA.

Blackfriars Road

Southwark

Tooley St.

The Tower

RIVER THAMES

Wapping

Rotherhithe Tunnel

94
St. James's Park

Whitehall

95

96

LONDON BRIDGE STA.

97

Bridge Road

98
Jamaica Road

99
Lower Road
A200

Mall

Lambeth

Lambeth Road

Kennington Road

A3

A201

Tower Bridge Road
A2

Bermondsey

Southwark Park

Westminster

Bridge Road

Albert Embankment

104
105

Elms Lane

Kennington Road

A215

Old Kent Road
A2

Rotherhithe New Road

ΓHAMES

Wandsworth Road

Clapham Road

Brixton Road

Camberwell New Road
A202

Kennington

Camberwell Road

Peckham Road

A202

Queen's Road

Peckham

A2,M2
and Dover

Guildford and Portsmouth / A3

A23
Gatwick Airport and Brighton

0   1   2
Miles

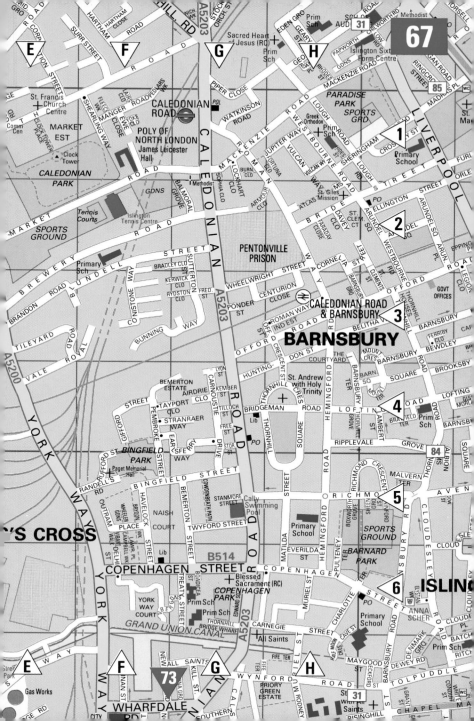

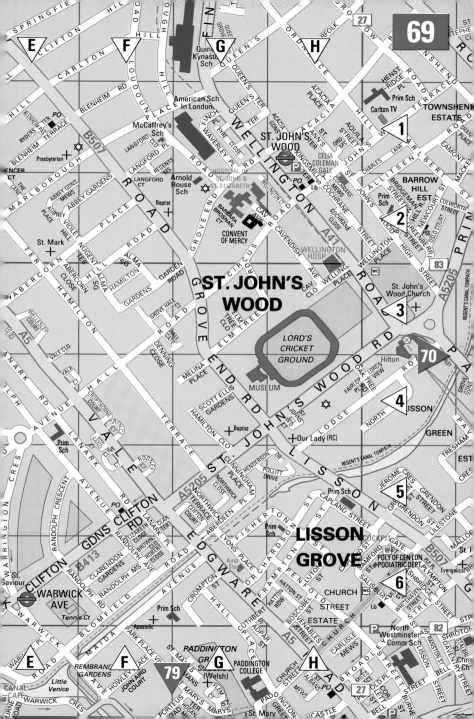

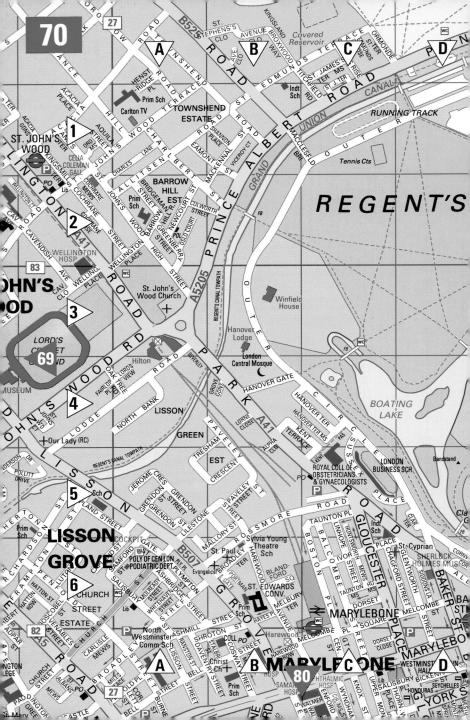

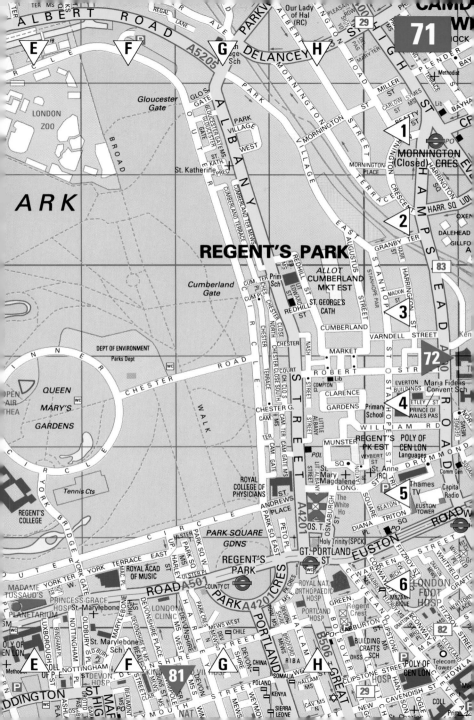

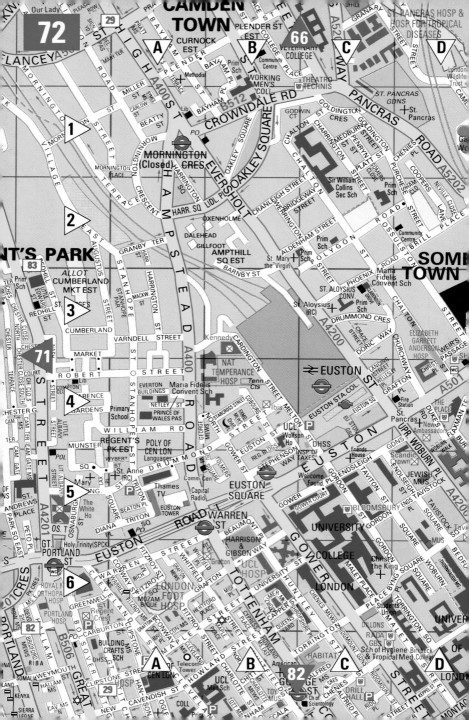

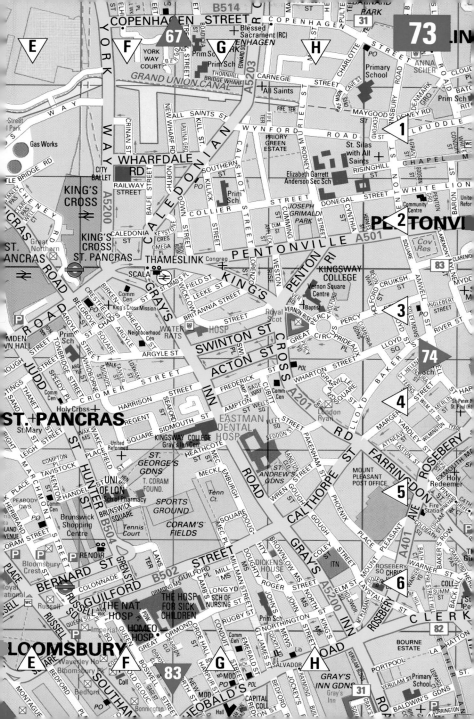

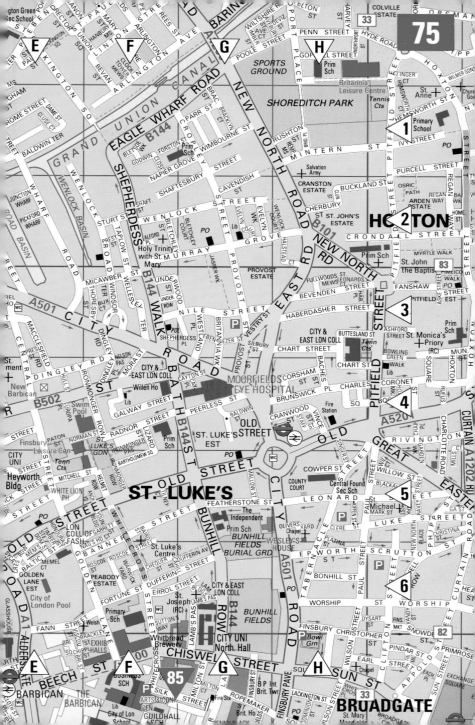

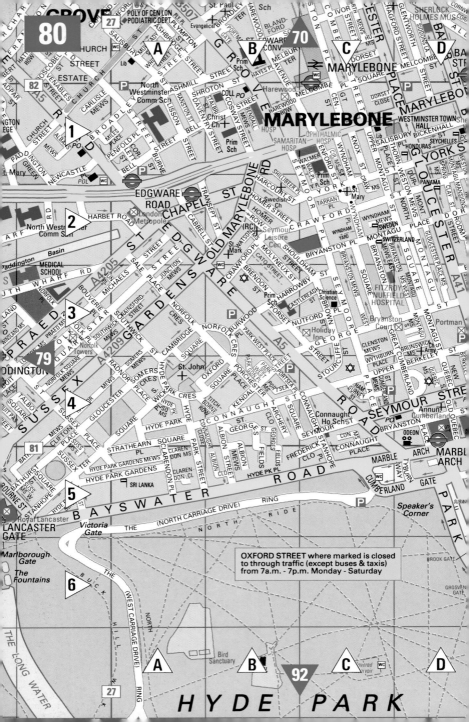

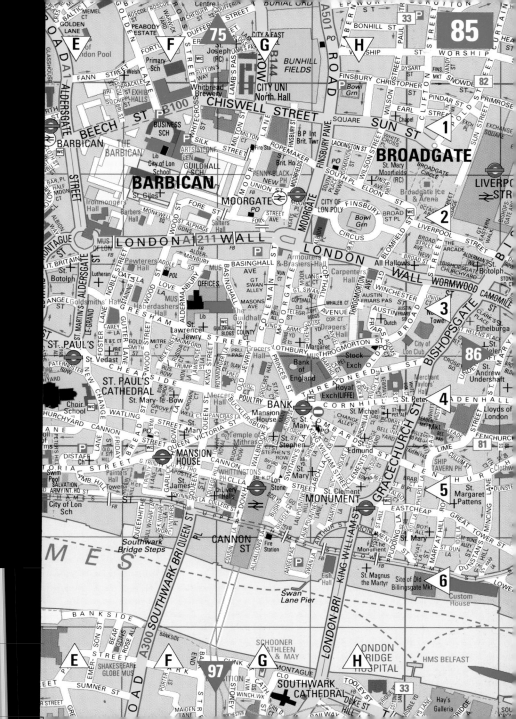

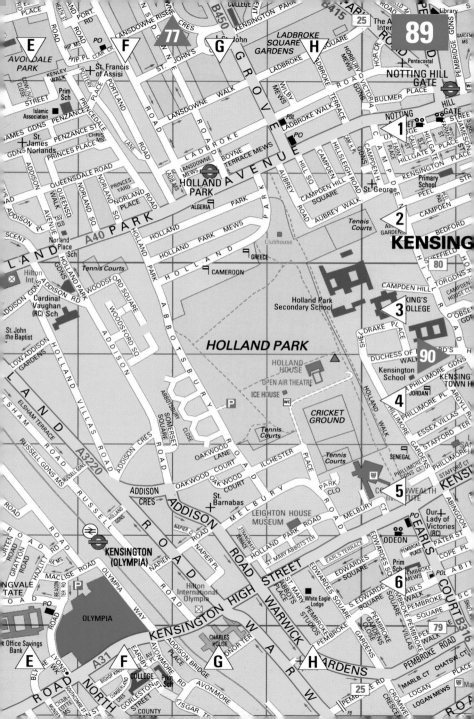

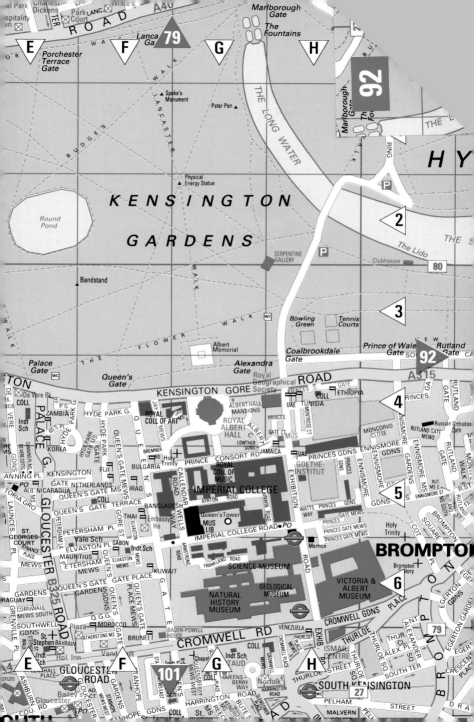

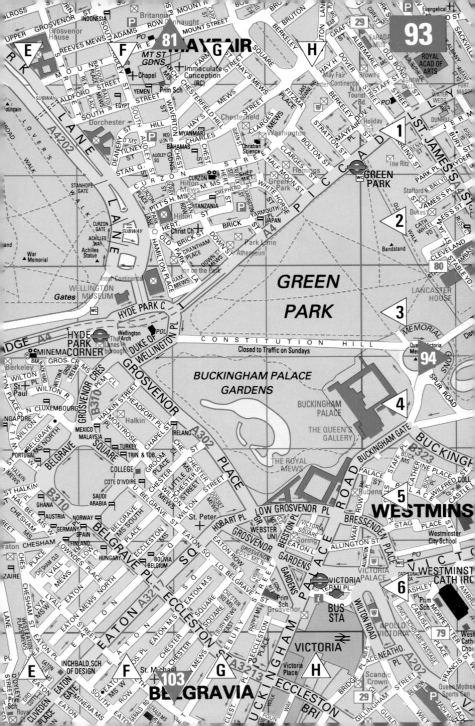

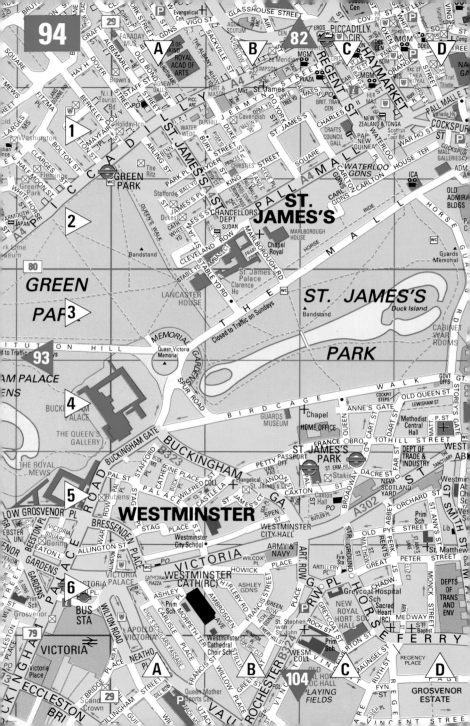

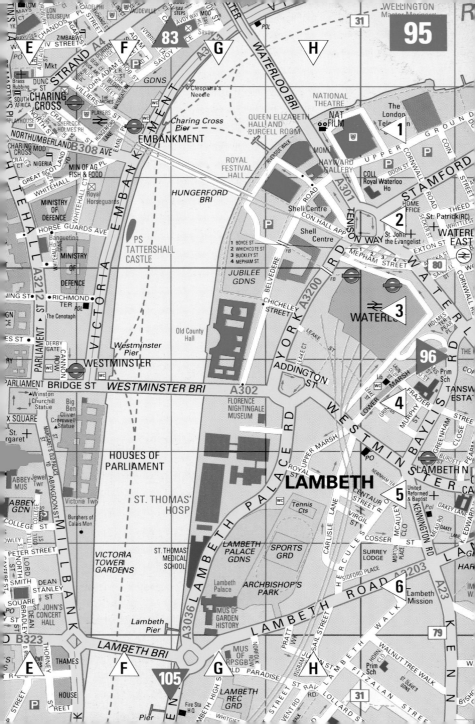

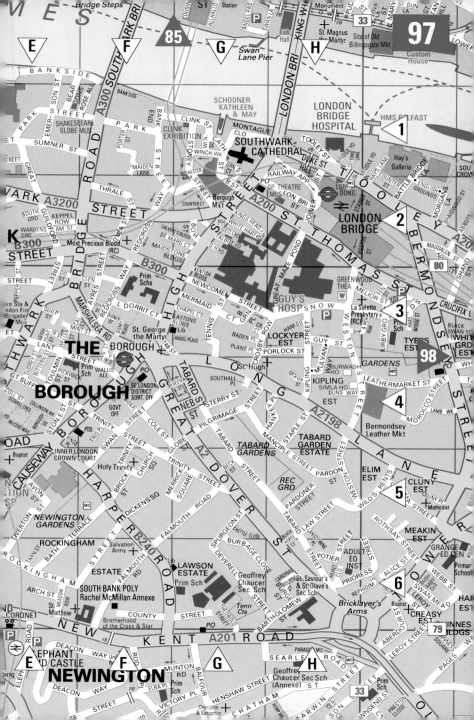

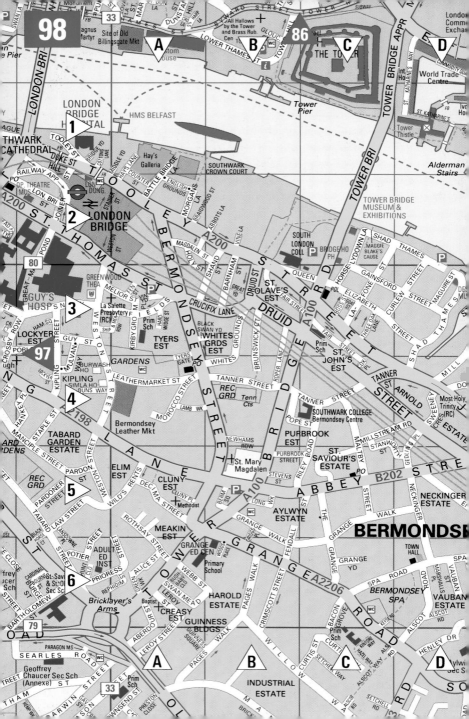

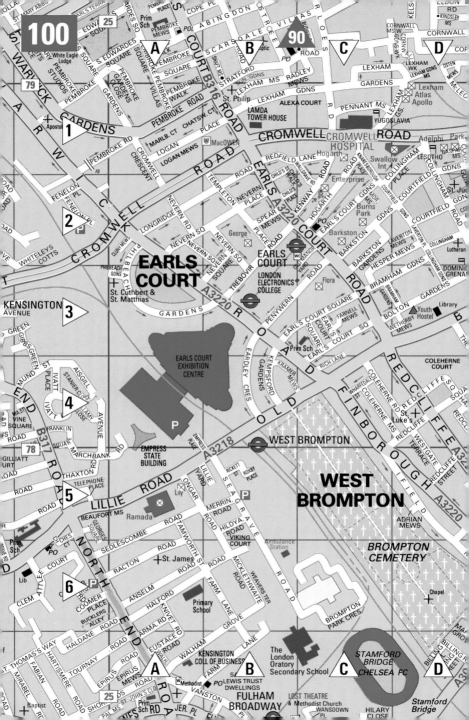

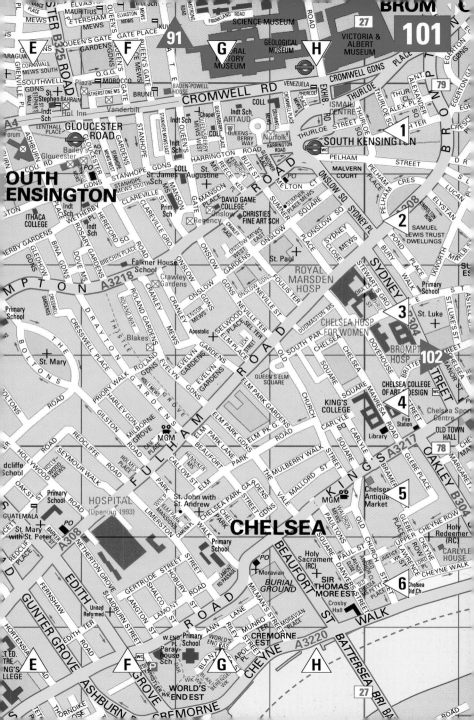

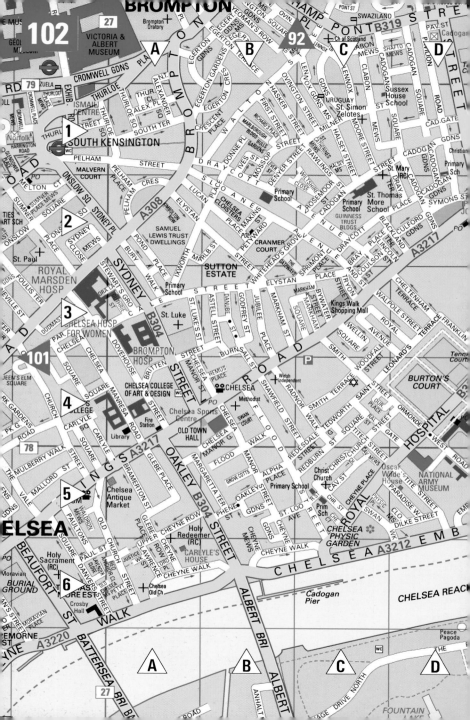

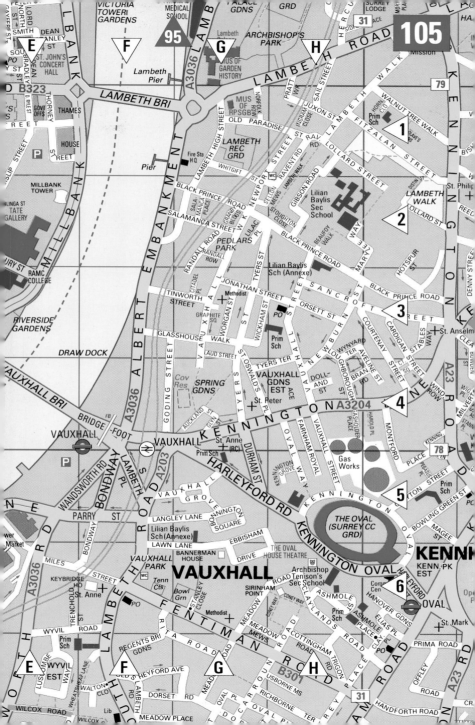

INDEX TO STREETS

General Abbreviations

All	Alley	Embk	Embankment	Pk	Park
Allot	Allotments	Est	Estate	Pl	Place
Amb	Ambulance	FB	Footbridge	Prec	Precinct
App	Approach	Flds	Fields	Prim	Primary
Arc	Arcade	Fm	Farm	Pt	Point
Ave	Avenue	Gall	Gallery	RC	Roman Catholic
Bdy	Broadway	Gar	Garage	Rd	Road
Bldgs	Buildings	Gdn	Garden	Rec	Recreation
Bowl	Bowling	Gdns	Gardens	Resr	Reservoir
Bri	Bridge	Govt	Government	Ri	Rise
C of E	Church of England	Grd	Ground	S	South
Cath	Cathedral	Grn	Green	Sch	School
Cen	Central, Centre	Gro	Grove	Sec	Secondary
Ch	Church	Ho	House	Sq	Square
Chyd	Churchyard	Hosp	Hospital	St	Street
Circ	Circus	Ind	Industrial	St.	Saint
Clo	Close	Indt	Independent	Sta	Station
Co	County	La	Lane	Swim	Swimming
Coll	College	Lib	Library	TA	Territorial Army
Comm	Community	Lo	Lodge	Tenn	Tennis
Comp	Comprehensive	Mag	Magistrates	Ter	Terrace
Conv	Convent	Mans	Mansions	Thea	Theatre
Cor	Corner	Mkt	Market	Twr	Tower
Coron	Coroners	Ms	Mews	Vill	Villas
Cotts	Cottages	Mt	Mount	Vw	View
Cov	Covered	Mus	Museum	W	West
Cres	Crescent	N	North	Wd	Wood
Ct	Court	Off	Office	Wf	Wharf
Dr	Drive	PH	Public House	Wk	Walk
Dws	Dwellings	Par	Parade	Wks	Works
E	East	Pas	Passage		
Ed	Education	Pav	Pavilion		

NOTES

The figures and letters following a street name indicate the Postal District, page and map square where the name can be found.

Name	Page	Ref
Clarges Ms. W1	93	G1
Clarges St. W1	93	H1
Clark St. E1	87	H2
Clarke's Ms. W1	81	F1
Clarks Pl. EC2	86	A3
Claverton St. SW1	104	B4
Claxton Gro. W6	52	D4
Clay St. W1	80	D2
Claybrook Rd. W6	52	D5
Claylands Rd. SW8	105	H6
Clearwell Dr. W9	68	D6
Clegg St. E1	99	H1
Clem Attlee Ct. SW6	53	H6
Clement's Inn WC2	83	H4
Clement's Inn Pas. WC2	83	H4
Clements La. EC4	85	H5
Clements Rd. SE16	99	F6
Clenham St. SE1	97	F3
Clenston Ms. W1	80	C3
Clere St. EC2	75	H5
Clerkenwell Clo. EC1	74	B5
Clerkenwell Grn. EC1	74	B6
Clerkenwell Rd. EC1	74	A6
Cleveland Gdns. W2	79	E4
Cleveland Ms. W1	82	A1
Cleveland Pl. SW1	94	B1
Cleveland Row SW1	94	A2
Cleveland Sq. W2	79	E4
Cleveland St. W1	71	H6
Cleveland Ter. W2	79	E4
Cliff Rd. NW1	66	D1
Cliff Vill. NW1	66	D1
Clifford St. W1	82	A6
Clifton Ct. NW8	69	G5
Clifton Gdns. W9	69	E6
Clifton Hill NW8	68	D1
Clifton Pl. W2	79	H4
Clifton Rd. W9	69	F5
Clifton St. EC2	86	A1
Clifton Vills. W9	78	D1
Clink St. SE1	97	G1
Clipstone Ms. W1	72	A6
Clipstone St. W1	81	H1
Clive Ct. W9	69	F5
Clivedon Pl. SW1	103	E1
Cloak La. EC4	85	G5
Clock Tower Pl. N7	67	E1
Cloth Ct. EC1	84	D2
Cloth Fair EC1	84	D2
Cloth St. EC1	85	E1
Clover Ms. SW3	102	D5
Cloysters Clo. E1	99	E1
Clunbury St. N1	75	H2
Cluny Est. SE1	98	A5
Cluny Ms. SW5	100	A2
Cluny Pl. SE1	98	A5
Cluse Ct. N1	75	E1
Clydesdale Rd. W11	77	G3
Coach & Horses Yd. W1	82	A5
Cobb St. E1	86	C2
Cobourg St. NW1	72	B4
Coburg Clo. SW1	104	B1
Cochrane Clo. NW8	69	H2
Cochrane Ms. NW8	69	H2
Cochrane St. NW8	69	H2
Cock Hill E1	86	B2
Cock La. EC1	84	C2
Cockpit Steps SW1	94	D4
Cockpit Yd. WC1	83	H1
Cockspur Ct. SW1	94	D1
Cockspur St. SW1	94	D1
Codling Clo. E1	99	F1
Codrington Ms. W11	77	F4
Coin St. SE1	96	A1
Coke St. E1	87	E3
Colbeck Ms. SW7	100	D2
Colchester St. E1	86	D3
Coldbath Sq. EC1	74	A5
Cole St. SE1	97	F4
Colebrooke Row N1	74	C2
Coleherne Ms. SW5	100	D4
Coleherne Ms. SW10	100	C4
Coleherne Rd. SW10	100	C4
Coleman St. EC2	85	G3
Colet Gdns. W14	52	D2
Coley St. WC1	73	H6
College Gro. NW1	66	C6
College Hill EC4	85	F5
College Ms. SW1	95	E5
College Pl. NW1	66	B5
College St. EC4	85	G5
Collett Rd. SE16	99	F6
Collier St. N1	73	G2
Collingham Gdns. SW5	100	D2
Collingham Pl. SW5	100	C2
Collingham Rd. SW5	100	D1
Collinson St. SE1	97	E4
Collinson Wk. SE1	97	E4
Colnbrook St. SE1	96	C6
Colombo St. SE1	96	C2
Colonade Wk. SW1	103	G2
Colonnade WC1	73	F6
Colonnades, The W2	78	D3
Colville Gdns. W11	77	H4
Colville Houses W11	77	G3
Colville Ms. W11	77	H4
Colville Pl. W1	82	B2
Colville Rd. W11	77	H4
Colville Sq. W11	77	G4
Colville Ter. W11	77	G4
Colwith Rd. W6	52	B6
Comeragh Ms. W14	53	F3
Comeragh Rd. W14	53	F4
Commercial Rd. E1	87	E3
Commodity Quay E1	86	D6
Compton Clo. NW1	71	H4
Compton Pas. EC1	74	D5
Compton Pl. WC1	73	E6
Compton St. EC1	74	C5
Conant Ms. E1	87	E3
Concert Hall App. SE1	95	H2
Conduit Ct. WC2	83	E5
Conduit Ms. W2	79	G4
Conduit Pas. W2	79	G4
Conduit Pl. W2	79	G4
Conduit St. W1	81	H5
Coney Way SW8	105	H6
Conistone Way N7	67	F3
Connaught Clo. W2	80	A4
Connaught Ms. W2	80	C4
Connaught Pl. W2	80	C4
Connaught Sq. W2	80	C4
Connaught St. W2	80	B4
Cons St. SE1	96	B3
Constitution Hill SW1	93	G3
Convent Gdns. W11	77	F4
Conway Ms. W1	72	A6
Conway St. W1	72	A6
Coombs St. N1	74	D2
Coomer Ms. SW6	53	H6
Coomer Pl. SW6	53	H6
Coomer Rd. SW6	53	H6
Cooper Clo. SE1	96	B4
Coopers La. NW1	72	D2
Coopers Row EC3	86	C5
Cope Pl. W8	90	A6
Copenhagen St. N1	67	F6
Copperfield St. SE1	96	D3
Copthall Ave. EC2	85	H3
Copthall Bldgs. EC2	85	H3
Copthall Clo. EC2	85	G3
Copthall Ct. EC2	85	H3
Coptic St. WC1	83	E2
Coral St. SE1	96	B4
Coram St. WC1	73	E6
Corbet Ct. EC3	85	H4
Corbet Pl. E1	86	C1
Cork Sq. E1	99	G1
Cork St. W1	82	A6
Cork St. Ms. W1	82	A6
Corlett St. NW1	80	A1
Cornelia St. N7	67	H2
Corner House St. WC2	95	E1
Cornhill EC3	85	H4
Cornwall Cres. W11	77	E5
Cornwall Gdns. SW7	90	D6
Cornwall Gdns. Wk. SW7	90	D6
Cornwall Ms. S. SW7	91	E6
Cornwall Ms. W. SW7	90	D6
Cornwall Rd. SE1	96	A1
Cornwall St. E1	87	H5
Cornwall Ter. NW1	70	D6
Cornwall Ter. Ms. NW1	70	D6
Corporation Row EC1	74	B5
Corsham St. N1	75	H4
Cosmo Pl. WC1	83	F1
Cosser St. SE1	96	A5
Cosway St. NW1	80	B1
Cottage Pl. SW3	92	A6
Cottesmore Gdns. W8	90	D5
Cottons La. SE1	97	H1
Coulson St. SW3	102	D3
Counter Ct. SE1	97	G2
Counter St. SE1	98	A2
County St. SE1	97	F6
Court St. E1	87	G1
Courtfield Gdns. SW5	100	D2
Courtfield Ms. SW5	100	D2
Courtfield Rd. SW7	101	E1
Courtnell St. W2	78	A3
Courtyard, The N1	67	H3
Cousin La. EC4	85	G6
Covent Gdn. WC2	83	F5
Coventry St. W1	82	C6
Coverley Clo. E1	87	F1
Cowcross St. EC1	84	C1
Cowdenbeath Path N1	67	G5
Cowley St. SW1	95	E5
Cowling Clo. W11	89	E1
Cowper St. EC2	75	H5
Cowper Ter. W10	76	C2
Coxson Pl. SE1	98	C4
Crace St. NW1	72	C3
Craigs Ct. SW1	95	E1
Cramer St. W1	81	F2
Cramond Clo. W6	53	E6
Cranbourn All. WC2	82	D5
Cranbourn St. WC2	82	D5
Crane Ct. EC4	84	B4
Cranfield Row SE1	96	B5
Cranleigh St. NW1	72	B2
Cranley Gdns. SW7	101	F3
Cranley Ms. SW7	101	F3
Cranley Pl. SW7	101	G2
Cranmer Ct. SW3	102	B2
Cranston St. N1	75	H2
Cranwood St. EC1	75	H4
Craven Hill W2	79	F5
Craven Hill Gdns. W2	79	E5
Craven Hill Ms. W2	79	F5
Craven Pas. WC2	95	E1
Craven Rd. W2	79	F5
Craven St. WC2	95	E1
Craven Ter. W2	79	F5
Crawford Ms. W1	80	C2
Crawford Pas. EC1	74	A6
Crawford Pl. W1	80	B2
Crawford St. W1	80	B2
Creasy Est. SE1	98	A6
Creechurch La. EC3	86	B4
Creechurch Pl. EC3	86	B4
Creed La. EC4	84	D4
Crefeld Clo. W6	53	E6
Crescent, The EC3	86	C5
Crescent Pl. SW3	102	A1
Crescent Row EC1	75	E6
Crescent St. N1	67	H3
Cresswell Gdns. SW5	101	E3
Cresswell Pl. SW10	101	E3
Crestfield St. WC1	73	F3
Crimscott St. SE1	98	B6
Crinan St. N1	73	F1
Cripplegate St. EC2	85	E1
Crisp Rd. W6	52	A4
Crispin St. E1	86	C2
Crofters Way NW1	66	C5
Crofts St. E1	87	E6
Cromer St. WC1	73	F4
Crompton St. W2	69	G6
Cromwell Clo. E1	99	F1
Cromwell Cres. SW5	100	A1
Cromwell Gdns. SW7	91	H6

M

Name	Page	Grid
Randolph Rd. W9	69	E6
Randolph St. NW1	66	B4
Ranelagh Gro. SW1	103	F3
Ranelagh Rd. SW1	104	B4
Rannoch Rd. W6	52	B5
Ranston St. NW1	80	A1
Raphael St. SW7	92	C4
Rathbone Pl. W1	82	C2
Rathbone St. W1	82	B2
Raven Row E1	87	H1
Ravent Rd. SE11	105	H1
Rawlings St. SW3	102	C1
Rawstorne Pl. EC1	74	C3
Rawstorne St. EC1	74	C3
Ray St. EC1	74	B6
Ray St. Bri. EC1	74	B6
Raymond Bldgs. WC1	83	H1
Reachview Clo. NW1	66	B4
Reapers Clo. NW1	66	C5
Reardon Path E1	99	H2
Reardon St. E1	99	G1
Red Anchor Clo. SW3	102	A6
Red Lion Ct. EC4	84	B4
Red Lion Sq. WC1	83	G2
Red Lion St. WC1	83	G1
Red Lion Yd. W1	93	F1
Redan Pl. W2	78	C4
Redan St. W14	88	D5
Redburn St. SW3	102	C5
Redcliffe Gdns. SW10	100	D4
Redcliffe Ms. SW10	100	D4
Redcliffe Pl. SW10	101	E6
Redcliffe Rd. SW10	101	E4
Redcliffe Sq. SW10	100	D4
Redcliffe St. SW10	100	D5
Redcross Way SE1	97	F3
Rede Pl. W2	78	B5
Redesdale St. SW3	102	B5
Redfield La. SW5	100	B1
Redhill St. NW1	71	H3
Redmead La. E1	99	E2
Reece Ms. SW7	101	G1
Reeds Pl. NW1	66	A3
Reeves Ms. W1	81	E6
Regal Clo. E1	87	F1
Regency Pl. SW1	104	D1
Regency St. SW1	104	D1
Regent Pl. W1	82	B5
Regent Sq. WC1	73	F4
Regent St. SW1	82	C6
Regent St. W1	81	H3
Regents Ms. NW8	69	F1
Regents Park NW1	70	C2
Regents Park Est. NW1	72	A4
Regnart Bldgs. NW1	72	B5
Relay Rd. W12	76	B6
Relton Ms. SW7	92	B5
Rembrandt Clo. SW1	103	E2
Remington St. N1	74	D2
Remnant St. WC2	83	G3
Rempstone Ms. N1	75	H1
Rennie St. SE1	96	C1
Rephidim St. SE1	97	H6
Reston Pl. SW7	91	E4
Reunion Row E1	87	H6
Rex Pl. W1	81	F6
Rheidol Ms. N1	75	E1
Rheidol Ter. N1	74	D1
Rich La. SW5	100	C4
Richard St. E1	87	G4
Richards Pl. SW3	102	B1
Richardson's Ms. W1	72	A6
Richbell Pl. WC1	83	G1
Richford St. W6	88	A4
Richmond Ave. N1	67	H5
Richmond Bldgs. W1	82	C4
Richmond Cres. E4	67	H5
Richmond Ms. W1	82	C4
Richmond Ter. SW1	95	E3
Richmond Way W12	88	D3
Richmond Way W14	88	D4
Rickett St. SW6	100	B5
Ridgmount Gdns. WC1	82	C1
Ridgmount Pl. WC1	82	C1
Ridgmount St. WC1	82	C1
Riding House St. W1	81	H2
Rifle Pl. W11	88	D1
Riley Rd. SE1	98	C5
Ring, The W2	80	A5
Ripplevale Gro. N1	67	H4
Risborough St. SE1	96	D3
Rising Sun Ct. EC1	84	D2
Risinghill St. N1	74	A1
Rita Rd. SW8	105	F6
Ritchie St. N1	74	B1
River St. EC1	74	A3
River Ter. W6	52	A4
Riverside Ct. SW8	104	D5
Riverside Wk. SE1	95	H1
Robert Adam St. W1	81	E3
Robert Clo. W9	69	F6
Robert Gentry Ho. W14	53	E4
Robert St. NW1	71	H4
Robert St. WC2	83	F6
Roberts Ms. SW1	93	E6
Robert's Pl. EC1	74	B5
Robinson St. SW3	102	C5
Rochester Ms. NW1	66	A3
Rochester Pl. NW1	66	A2
Rochester Rd. NW1	66	A2
Rochester Row SW1	104	B1
Rochester Sq. NW1	66	B3
Rochester St. SW1	94	C6
Rochester Ter. NW1	66	A2
Rochester Wk. SE1	97	G1
Rockingham Est. SE1	97	E6
Rockingham St. SE1	97	E6
Rockley Rd. W14	88	C3
Rockwood Pl. W12	88	B3
Rocliffe St. N1	74	D2
Roding Ms. E1	99	F1
Rodmarton St. W1	80	D2
Rodney Ct. W9	69	F5
Rodney St. N1	73	H1
Roger St. WC1	73	H6
Roland Gdns. SW7	101	F3
Roland Way SW7	101	F3
Rolls Bldgs. EC4	84	A3
Rolls Pas. EC4	84	A3
Roman Way N7	67	G1
Roman Way Ind. Est. N1	67	H3
Romford St. E1	87	F2
Romilly St. W1	82	C5
Romney St. SW1	95	E6
Rood La. EC3	86	A5
Rope Walk Gdns. E1	87	F3
Ropemaker St. EC2	85	G1
Roper La. SE1	98	B4
Rosary Gdns. SW7	101	E2
Roscoe St. EC1	75	F6
Rose Alley SE1	97	F1
Rose & Crown Ct. EC2	85	E3
Rose & Crown Yd. SW1	94	B1
Rose St. WC2	83	E5
Rosebank Wk. NW1	66	D3
Rosebery Ave. EC1	74	A5
Rosebery Sq. EC1	74	A6
Rosedew Rd. W6	52	C6
Roseford Ct. W12	88	C4
Rosehart Ms. W11	78	A4
Rosemoor St. SW3	102	C2
Rosmead Rd. W11	77	F5
Rosoman Pl. EC1	74	B5
Rosoman St. EC1	74	B4
Rossendale Way NW1	66	B4
Rossmore Rd. NW1	70	B6
Rotary St. SE1	96	C5
Rotherham Wk. SE1	96	C2
Rothsay St. SE1	98	A5
Rotten Row SW1	92	C3
Rotten Row SW7	92	B3
Rouel Rd. SE16	99	E6
Roupell St. SE1	96	B2
Rousden St. NW1	66	A4
Rowan Rd. W6	52	C2
Rowan Ter. W6	52	C1
Rowington Clo. W2	78	C1
Rowstock Gdns. N7	66	D1
Roxby Pl. SW6	100	B5
Royal Arc. W1	82	A6
Royal Ave. SW3	102	C3
Royal College St. NW1	66	A3
Royal Cres. W11	88	D2
Royal Cres. Ms. W11	88	D2
Royal Exchange EC3	85	H4
Royal Exchange Ave. EC3	85	H4
Royal Exchange Bldgs. EC3	85	H4
Royal Hospital Rd. SW3	102	C5
Royal Mint Pl. E1	86	D5
Royal Mint St. E1	86	D5
Royal Opera Arc. SW1	94	C1
Royal St. SE1	95	H5
Royalty Ms. W1	82	C4
Rudolph Rd. NW6	68	B2
Rufford St. N1	67	F5
Rugby St. WC1	73	G6
Runcorn Pl. W11	77	E5
Rupert Ct. W1	82	C5
Rupert St. W1	82	C5
Rushton St. N1	75	H1
Rushworth St. SE1	96	D3
Russell Ct. SW1	94	B2
Russell Gdns. W14	89	E5
Russell Gdns. Ms. W14	89	E5
Russell Rd. W14	89	F5
Russell Sq. WC1	73	E6
Russell St. WC2	83	F5
Russia Ct. EC2	85	F4
Russia Row EC2	85	F4
Ruston Ms. W11	77	E4
Rutherford St. SW1	104	C1
Rutland Gdns. SW7	92	B4
Rutland Gdns. Ms. SW7	92	B4
Rutland Gate SW7	92	B4
Rutland Gate Ms. SW7	92	A4
Rutland Ms. E. SW7	92	A5
Rutland Ms. S. SW7	92	A5
Rutland Pl. EC1	84	D1
Rutland St. SW7	92	B5
Ryder Ct. SW1	94	B1
Ryder St. SW1	94	B1
Ryder Yd. SW1	94	B1
Ryders Ter. NW8	69	E1
Rydston Clo. N7	67	G3
Rylston Rd. SW6	53	G6
Rysbrack St. SW3	92	C5

Name	Page	Grid
Sackville St. W1	82	B6
Saffron Hill EC1	84	B1
Saffron St. EC1	84	B1
Sage Way WC1	73	G4
Sail St. SE11	105	H1
St. Albans Gro. W8	90	D5
St. Albans Ms. W2	79	H1
St. Albans St. SW1	82	C6
St. Albans Ter. W6	53	E5
St. Alphage Gdns. EC2	85	F2
St. Andrew St. EC4	84	B2
St. Andrew's Hill EC4	84	D5
St. Andrews Pl. NW1	71	H5
St. Andrews Rd. W14	53	F5
St. Andrews Sq. W11	77	E4
St. Anne's Ct. W1	82	C4
St. Ann's La. SW1	94	D5
St. Anns Rd. W11	76	D6
St. Ann's St. SW1	94	D5
St. Ann's Ter. NW8	69	H1
St. Anns Vill. W11	88	D2
St. Anselms Pl. W1	81	G4
St. Anthonys Clo. E1	99	E1
St. Augustines Rd. NW1	66	C3
St. Barnabas St. SW1	103	F3
St. Benet's Pl. EC3	85	H5
St. Botolph Row EC3	86	C4
St. Botolph St. EC3	86	C3
St. Bride St. EC4	84	C3
St. Bride's Pas. EC4	84	C4

Sidmouth St. WC1	73	F4
Sidney Gro. EC1	74	C2
Sidney St. E1	87	H1
Silbury St. N1	75	G3
Silchester Rd. W10	76	D4
Silex St. SE1	96	D4
Silk St. EC2	85	F1
Silver Pl. W1	82	B5
Silver Rd. W12	76	C6
Silverton Rd. W6	52	C6
Silvester St. SE1	97	G4
Simla Ho. SE1	97	H4
Simon Clo. W11	77	H5
Sinclair Gdns. W14	88	D4
Sinclair Rd. W14	88	D4
Singer St. EC2	75	H4
Sir Thomas More Est. SW3	101	H6
Sirdar Rd. W11	76	D6
Sirinham Point SW8	105	G6
Sise La. EC4	85	G4
Skelwith Rd. W6	52	B6
Skinner Pl. SW1	103	E2
Skinner St. EC1	74	B4
Skinners La. EC4	85	F5
Skipton St. SE1	96	D6
Slaidburn St. SW10	101	F6
Slingsby Pl. WC2	83	E5
Slippers Pl. SE16	99	H5
Sloane Ave. SW3	102	B2
Sloane Ct. E. SW3	103	E3
Sloane Ct. W. SW3	103	E3
Sloane Gdns. SW1	103	E2
Sloane Sq. SW1	102	D2
Sloane St. SW1	92	D5
Sloane Ter. SW1	102	D1
Sly St. E1	87	G4
Smallbrook Ms. W2	79	G4
Smart's Pl. WC2	83	F3
Smeaton St. E1	99	G1
Smith Sq. SW1	95	E6
Smith St. SW3	102	C3
Smith Ter. SW3	102	C4
Smithfield St. EC1	84	C2
Smith's Ct. W1	82	B5
Snarsgate St. W10	76	B2
Snow Hill EC1	84	C2
Snow Hill Ct. EC1	84	D3
Snowsfields SE1	97	H3
Soho Sq. W1	82	C3
Soho St. W1	82	C3
Soley Ms. WC1	74	A3
Somers Clo. NW1	72	C1
Somers Cres. W2	80	A4
Somers Ms. W2	80	A4
Somerset Sq. W14	89	F4
Sophia Clo. N7	67	G1
Souldern Rd. W14	88	D6
South Audley St. W1	81	F6
South Bolton Gdns. SW5	100	D3
South Carriage Dr. SW7	92	A3
South Cres. WC1	82	C2
South Eaton Pl. SW1	103	F1
South Edwardes Sq. W8	89	H6
South End W8	90	D5
South End Row W8	90	D5
South Lambeth Pl. SW8	105	F5
South Molton La. W1	81	G4
South Molton St. W1	81	G4
South Par. SW3	101	H3
South Pl. EC2	85	H2
South Pl. Ms. EC2	85	H2
South Sq. WC1	84	A2
South St. W1	93	F1
South Tenter St. E1	86	D4
South Ter. SW7	102	A1
South Vill. NW1	66	D2
South Wharf Rd. W2	79	G3
Southall Pl. SE1	97	G4
Southampton Bldgs. WC2	84	A2
Southampton Pl. WC1	83	F2
Southampton Row WC1	83	F1
Southampton St. WC2	83	F5
Southcombe St. W14	53	E1
Southern St. N1	73	G1

Southerton Rd. W6	88	A6
Southwark Bri. EC4	85	F6
Southwark Bri. SE1	85	F6
Southwark Bri. Rd. SE1	97	E4
Southwark Gro. SE1	97	E2
Southwark St. SE1	96	D1
Southwell Gdns. SW7	91	E6
Southwick Ms. W2	79	H3
Southwick Pl. W2	80	A4
Southwick St. W2	80	A3
Sovereign Clo. E1	87	H6
Spa Green Est. EC1	74	B3
Spa Rd. SE16	98	C6
Spafield St. EC1	74	A5
Spanish Pl. W1	81	F3
Spear Ms. SW5	100	B2
Speedy Pl. WC1	73	E4
Spelman St. E1	87	E1
Spencer Ct. NW8	69	E1
Spencer Ms. W6	53	E5
Spencer St. EC1	74	C4
Spenser St. SW1	94	B5
Spirit Quay E1	99	F1
Spital Sq. E1	86	B1
Spital Yd. E1	86	B1
Sprimont Pl. SW3	102	C3
Spring Gdns. SW1	94	D1
Spring Ms. W1	80	D1
Spring St. W2	79	G4
Spring Wk. E1	87	F1
Springbank Wk. NW1	66	D3
Springvale Est. W14	89	E6
Springvale Ter. W14	88	D6
Spur Rd. SW1	94	A4
Spurgeon St. SE1	97	G6
Square, The W6	52	B4
Stable Way W10	76	B4
Stable Yd. SW1	94	A3
Stable Yd. Rd. SW1	94	B3
Stacey St. WC2	82	D4
Stackhouse St. SW3	92	C5
Staff St. EC1	75	H4
Stafford Clo. NW6	68	A4
Stafford Pl. SW1	94	A5
Stafford Rd. NW6	68	A3
Stafford St. W1	94	A1
Stafford Ter. W8	90	A5
Stag Pl. SW1	94	A5
Stainer St. SE1	97	H2
Staining La. EC2	85	F3
Stalbridge St. NW1	80	B1
Stalham St. SE16	99	H6
Stamford St. SE1	96	A2
Stanford Rd. W8	90	D5
Stanford St. SW1	104	C2
Stanhope Gdns. SW7	101	F1
Stanhope Gate W1	93	F1
Stanhope Ms. E. SW7	101	F1
Stanhope Ms. S. SW7	101	F2
Stanhope Ms. W. SW7	101	F1
Stanhope Par. NW1	72	A3
Stanhope Pl. W2	80	C4
Stanhope Row W1	93	G2
Stanhope St. NW1	72	A3
Stanhope Ter. W2	79	H5
Stanier Clo. W14	53	H4
Stanlake Ms. W12	88	A2
Stanlake Rd. W12	88	A2
Stanlake Vill. W12	88	A2
Stanley Clo. SW8	105	G6
Stanley Cres. W11	77	G5
Stanley Gdns. W11	77	G5
Stanley Gardens Ms. W11	77	H5
Stanley Pas. NW1	73	E2
Stanmore St. N1	67	G5
Stanwick Rd. W14	53	G2
Stanworth St. SE1	98	C4
Staple Inn Bldgs. WC1	84	A2
Staple St. SE1	97	H4
Star Rd. W14	53	G5
Star St. W2	79	H3
Star Yd. WC2	84	A3
Starcross St. NW1	72	B4
Stedham Pl. WC1	83	E3

Stephen Ms. W1	82	C2
Stephen St. W1	82	C2
Stephenson Way NW1	72	B5
Stepney Way E1	87	G2
Sterling St. SW7	92	B4
Sterndale Rd. W14	88	C6
Sterne St. W12	88	C3
Sterry St. SE1	97	G4
Stevens St. SE1	98	B5
Steward St. E1	86	B1
Stewart's Gro. SW3	102	A3
Stillington St. SW1	104	B1
Stone Bldgs. WC2	83	H2
Stone House Ct. EC3	86	B3
Stonecutter St. EC4	84	C3
Stoneleigh Pl. W11	76	D6
Stoneleigh St. W11	76	D6
Stones End St. SE1	97	E4
Stoney La. E1	86	C3
Stoney St. SE1	97	G1
Stonor Rd. W14	53	G2
Store St. WC1	82	C2
Storeys Gate SW1	94	D4
Storks Rd. SE16	99	F6
Story St. N1	67	G4
Stothard Pl. EC2	86	B1
Stoughton Clo. SE11	105	H2
Stourcliffe St. W1	80	C4
Strand WC2	83	E6
Strand La. WC2	83	H5
Strangways Ter. W14	89	G5
Stranraer Way N1	67	F4
Stratford Ave. W8	90	B6
Stratford Pl. W1	81	G4
Stratford Rd. W8	90	B6
Stratford Vill. NW1	66	B3
Strathearn Pl. W2	80	A5
Strathmore Gdns. W8	90	B1
Stratton St. W1	93	H1
Streatham St. WC1	83	E3
Strutton Ground SW1	94	C5
Strype St. E1	86	C2
Stuart Rd. NW6	68	A4
Studio Pl. SW1	92	D4
Stukeley St. WC2	83	F3
Sturge St. SE1	97	E3
Sturt St. N1	75	F2
Stutfield St. E1	87	F4
Sudeley St. N1	74	D2
Sudrey St. SE1	97	E4
Suffolk La. EC4	85	G5
Suffolk Pl. SW1	94	D1
Suffolk St. SW1	82	D6
Sugar Bakers Ct. EC3	86	B4
Sulgrave Gdns. W6	88	B4
Sulgrave Rd. W6	88	B5
Summers St. EC1	74	A6
Sumner Pl. SW7	101	H2
Sumner Pl. Ms. SW7	101	H2
Sumner St. SE1	96	D1
Sun Ct. EC3	85	H4
Sun Pas. SE16	99	E5
Sun Rd. W14	53	G4
Sun St. EC2	85	H1
Sun St. Pas. EC2	86	A2
Sunderland Ter. W2	78	C3
Sunningdale Gdns. W8	90	B6
Surrendale Pl. W9	68	B6
Surrey Lo. SE1	96	A6
Surrey Row SE1	96	C3
Surrey St. WC2	83	H5
Sussex Gdns. W2	79	G5
Sussex Ms. E. W2	79	H4
Sussex Ms. W. W2	79	H5
Sussex Pl. NW1	70	C4
Sussex Pl. W2	79	H4
Sussex Pl. W6	52	B3
Sussex Sq. W2	79	H5
Sussex St. SW1	103	H4
Sutherland Ave. W9	68	B6
Sutherland Pl. W2	78	A3
Sutherland Row SW1	103	H3
Sutherland St. SW1	103	G3
Sutterton St. N7	67	G2

Upper Phillimore Gdns. W8	90	A4
Upper St. Martin's La. WC2	83	E5
Upper Tachbrook St. SW1	104	B1
Upper Thames St. EC4	84	D5
Upper Wimpole St. W1	81	F1
Upper Woburn Pl. WC1	72	D4
Uxbridge Rd. W12	88	A3
Uxbridge St. W8	90	A1

V

Vale, The SW3	101	G5
Vale Clo. W9	69	E4
Vale Ct. W9	69	E4
Vale Royal N7	67	E4
Valentine Pl. SE1	96	C3
Valentine Row SE1	96	C4
Vallance Rd. E1	87	F1
Vandon Pas. SW1	94	B5
Vandon St. SW1	94	B5
Vane St. SW1	104	B1
Varden St. E1	87	G3
Varndell St. NW1	72	A3
Vauban Est. SE16	98	D6
Vauban St. SE16	98	D6
Vaughan Way E1	87	E6
Vauxhall Bri. SE1	105	E4
Vauxhall Bri. SW1	105	E4
Vauxhall Bri. Rd. SW1	104	B1
Vauxhall Gdns. Est. SE11	105	H4
Vauxhall Gro. SW8	105	F5
Vauxhall St. SE11	105	H4
Vauxhall Wk. SE11	105	G3
Venables St. NW8	69	H6
Vere St. W1	81	G4
Vereker Rd. W14	53	F4
Verity Clo. W14	77	E4
Vernon Ms. W14	53	F2
Vernon Pl. WC1	83	F2
Vernon Ri. WC1	73	H3
Vernon Sq. WC1	73	H3
Vernon St. W14	53	E2
Vernon Yd. W11	77	G5
Verulam Bldgs. WC1	83	H1
Verulam St. WC1	84	A1
Vestry St. N1	75	G3
Vibart Wk. N1	67	F5
Vicarage Ct. W8	90	C3
Vicarage Gdns. W8	90	B2
Vicarage Gate W8	90	C3
Viceroy Ct. NW8	70	B1
Victoria Ave. EC2	86	B2
Victoria Embk. EC4	84	A5
Victoria Embk. SW1	95	F3
Victoria Embk. WC2	83	H6
Victoria Gdns. W11	88	A1
Victoria Gro. W8	91	E5
Victoria Grove Ms. W2	78	B6
Victoria Rd. W8	91	E4
Victoria Sq. SW1	93	H5
Victoria St. SW1	94	A6
Vigo St. W1	82	A6
Viking Ct. SW6	100	B5
Villiers St. WC2	95	F1
Vince St. EC1	75	H4
Vincent Sq. SW1	104	C1
Vincent St. SW1	104	C1
Vincent Ter. N1	74	C1
Vine Ct. E1	87	F2
Vine Hill EC1	74	A6
Vine La. SE1	98	B2
Vine Sq. W14	53	H4
Vine St. EC3	86	C4
Vine St. W1	82	B6
Vine Street Bri. EC1	74	B6
Vine Yd. SE1	97	F4
Vinegar St. E1	99	G1
Vinegar Yd. SE1	98	A3
Vineyard Wk. EC1	74	A5
Vintners Pl. EC4	85	F5
Violet Hill NW8	69	E2
Virgil Pl. W1	80	C2

Virgil St. SE1	95	H5
Virginia St. E1	87	F6
Viscount St. EC1	85	E1
Vulcan Way N7	67	H1

W

Waithman St. EC4	84	C4
Wakefield Ms. WC1	73	F4
Wakefield St. WC1	73	F4
Wakley St. EC1	74	C3
Walbrook EC4	85	G5
Walburgh St. E1	87	G4
Walcott St. SW1	104	B1
Walden St. E1	87	G3
Waldron Ms. SW3	101	H5
Walkers Ct. W1	82	C5
Wallgrave Rd. SW5	100	C1
Wallingford Ave. W10	76	C2
Wallis All. SE1	97	F4
Walmer Pl. W1	80	C1
Walmer Rd. W11	77	E5
Walmer St. W1	80	C1
Walpole St. SW3	102	C3
Walton Pl. SW3	92	C5
Walton St. SW3	102	B1
Wandsworth Rd. SW8	105	E5
Wapping Dock St. E1	99	H2
Wapping High St. E1	99	F2
Wapping La. E1	87	H6
Wardens Gro. SE1	97	E2
Wardour Ms. W1	82	B4
Wardour St. W1	82	B3
Wardrobe Pl. EC4	84	D4
Wardrobe Ter. EC4	84	D5
Warner St. EC1	74	A6
Warner Yd. EC1	74	A6
Warren Ms. W1	72	A6
Warren St. W1	71	H6
Warrington Cres. W9	69	E6
Warrington Gdns. W9	69	E6
Warwick Ave. W2	79	F1
Warwick Ave. W9	68	D6
Warwick Ct. WC1	83	H2
Warwick Cres. W2	79	E1
Warwick Est. W2	78	D2
Warwick Gdns. W14	89	H6
Warwick House St. SW1	94	D1
Warwick La. EC4	84	D4
Warwick Pl. W9	79	E1
Warwick Pl. N. SW1	104	A2
Warwick Rd. SW5	100	B3
Warwick Rd. W14	53	H1
Warwick Row SW1	93	H5
Warwick Sq. EC4	84	D3
Warwick Sq. SW1	104	A3
Warwick Sq. Ms. SW1	104	C2
Warwick St. W1	82	B5
Warwick Way SW1	103	H3
Warwick Yd. EC2	75	F6
Water St. WC2	83	H5
Watergate EC4	84	C5
Watergate Wk. WC2	83	F6
Waterhouse Clo. W6	52	D3
Waterloo Bridge SE1	83	G6
Waterloo Bridge WC2	83	G6
Waterloo Pl. SW1	94	C1
Waterloo Rd. SE1	96	A3
Waterman Way E1	99	G1
Waterside Clo. SE16	99	F4
Watkinson Rd. N7	67	G1
Watling Ct. EC4	85	F4
Watling St. EC4	85	E4
Watney Mkt. E1	87	H3
Watney St. E1	87	H4
Watson Ms. W1	80	B2
Watts St. E1	99	H1
Watts Way SW7	91	H5
Waveney Clo. E1	99	F1
Waverley Pl. NW8	69	G1
Waverley Wk. W2	78	B1
Waverton St. W1	93	G1

Waynflete Sq. W10	76	C4
Weavers Ter. SW6	100	B6
Weavers Way NW1	66	C4
Webb St. SE1	98	A6
Webber Row SE1	96	B4
Webber St. SE1	96	C4
Webster Rd. SE16	99	F6
Wedgwood Ms. W1	82	D4
Weighouse St. W1	81	F4
Weir's Pas. NW1	72	D3
Welbeck St. W1	81	F2
Welbeck Way W1	81	G3
Well Ct. EC4	85	F4
Welland Ms. E1	99	F1
Wellclose Sq. E1	87	F5
Wellclose St. E1	87	F6
Weller St. SE1	97	E3
Wellers Ct. NW1	73	E2
Wellesley Ct. W9	69	E3
Wellesley Pl. NW1	72	C4
Wellesley Ter. N1	75	F3
Wellington Bldgs. SW1	103	F4
Wellington Clo. W11	78	A4
Wellington Ct. NW8	69	G2
Wellington Pl. NW8	69	H3
Wellington Rd. NW8	69	G1
Wellington Sq. SW3	102	C3
Wellington Ter. WC2	83	F5
Wellington Ter. E1	99	G1
Wells Ms. W1	82	B2
Wells Rd. W12	88	A4
Wells Sq. WC1	73	G4
Wells St. W1	82	A2
Wells Way SW7	91	G5
Wenlock Ct. N1	75	H2
Wenlock Rd. N1	75	E2
Wenlock St. N1	75	F2
Wentworth St. E1	86	C3
Werrington St. NW1	72	B2
Wesley Sq. W11	77	E4
Wesley St. W1	81	F2
West Carriage Dr. W2	80	A6
West Central St. WC1	83	E3
West Cromwell Rd. SW5	100	A2
West Cromwell Rd. W14	53	G3
West Cross Route W10	76	C5
West Cross Route W11	76	C6
West Eaton Pl. SW1	103	E1
West Eaton Pl. Ms. SW1	93	E6
West Gdns. E1	87	H6
West Halkin St. SW1	93	E5
West Harding St. EC4	84	B3
West La. SE16	99	G4
West Mall W8	90	B1
West Ms. SW1	104	A2
West Pier E1	99	G2
West Poultry Ave. EC1	84	C2
West Rd. SW3	102	D4
West Smithfield EC1	84	C2
West Sq. SE11	96	C6
West St. WC2	82	D5
West Tenter St. E1	86	D4
West Warwick Pl. SW1	104	A2
Westbourne Bri. W2	79	E2
Westbourne Cres. W2	79	G5
Westbourne Cres. Ms. W2	79	G5
Westbourne Gdns. W2	78	C3
Westbourne Gro. W2	78	B4
Westbourne Gro. W11	77	G5
Westbourne Gro. Ms. W11	78	A4
Westbourne Gro. Ter. W2	78	C4
Westbourne Pk. Ms. W2	78	C3
Westbourne Pk. Pas. W2	78	B2
Westbourne Pk. Rd. W2	78	B2
Westbourne Pk. Rd. W11	77	F4
Westbourne Pk. Vill. W2	78	B2
Westbourne Rd. N7	67	H1
Westbourne St. W2	79	G5
Westbourne Ter. W2	79	F3
Westbourne Ter. Ms. W2	79	E3
Westbourne Ter. Rd. W2	79	E2
Westgate Ter. SW10	100	D4
Westland Pl. N1	75	G3
Westminster Bri. SE1	95	F4